DAN-78   DANTES SUBJECT STANDARDIZED TESTS (DSST)

This is your
PASSBOOK for...

Drug and Alcohol/ Substance Abuse

Test Preparation Study Guide
Questions & Answers

NATIONAL LEARNING CORPORATION®

COPYRIGHT NOTICE

This book is SOLELY intended for, is sold ONLY to, and its use is RESTRICTED to individual, bona fide applicants or candidates who qualify by virtue of having seriously filed applications for appropriate license, certificate, professional and/or promotional advancement, higher school matriculation, scholarship, or other legitimate requirements of education and/or governmental authorities.

This book is NOT intended for use, class instruction, tutoring, training, duplication, copying, reprinting, excerption, or adaptation, etc., by:

1) Other publishers
2) Proprietors and/or Instructors of "Coaching" and/or Preparatory Courses
3) Personnel and/or Training Divisions of commercial, industrial, and governmental organizations
4) Schools, colleges, or universities and/or their departments and staffs, including teachers and other personnel
5) Testing Agencies or Bureaus
6) Study groups which seek by the purchase of a single volume to copy and/or duplicate and/or adapt this material for use by the group as a whole without having purchased individual volumes for each of the members of the group
7) Et al.

Such persons would be in violation of appropriate Federal and State statutes.

PROVISION OF LICENSING AGREEMENTS – Recognized educational, commercial, industrial, and governmental institutions and organizations, and others legitimately engaged in educational pursuits, including training, testing, and measurement activities, may address request for a licensing agreement to the copyright owners, who will determine whether, and under what conditions, including fees and charges, the materials in this book may be used them. In other words, a licensing facility exists for the legitimate use of the material in this book on other than an individual basis. However, it is asseverated and affirmed here that the material in this book CANNOT be used without the receipt of the express permission of such a licensing agreement from the Publishers. Inquiries re licensing should be addressed to the company, attention rights and permissions department.

All rights reserved, including the right of reproduction in whole or in part, in any form or by any means, electronic or mechanical, including photocopying, recording, or by any information storage and retrieval system, without permission in writing from the Publisher.

Copyright © 2024 by
National Learning Corporation

212 Michael Drive, Syosset, NY 11791
(516) 921-8888 • www.passbooks.com
E-mail: info@passbooks.com

PUBLISHED IN THE UNITED STATES OF AMERICA

PASSBOOK® SERIES

THE *PASSBOOK® SERIES* has been created to prepare applicants and candidates for the ultimate academic battlefield – the examination room.

At some time in our lives, each and every one of us may be required to take an examination – for validation, matriculation, admission, qualification, registration, certification, or licensure.

Based on the assumption that every applicant or candidate has met the basic formal educational standards, has taken the required number of courses, and read the necessary texts, the *PASSBOOK® SERIES* furnishes the one special preparation which may assure passing with confidence, instead of failing with insecurity. Examination questions – together with answers – are furnished as the basic vehicle for study so that the mysteries of the examination and its compounding difficulties may be eliminated or diminished by a sure method.

This book is meant to help you pass your examination provided that you qualify and are serious in your objective.

The entire field is reviewed through the huge store of content information which is succinctly presented through a provocative and challenging approach – the question-and-answer method.

A climate of success is established by furnishing the correct answers at the end of each test.

You soon learn to recognize types of questions, forms of questions, and patterns of questioning. You may even begin to anticipate expected outcomes.

You perceive that many questions are repeated or adapted so that you can gain acute insights, which may enable you to score many sure points.

You learn how to confront new questions, or types of questions, and to attack them confidently and work out the correct answers.

You note objectives and emphases, and recognize pitfalls and dangers, so that you may make positive educational adjustments.

Moreover, you are kept fully informed in relation to new concepts, methods, practices, and directions in the field.

You discover that you are actually taking the examination all the time: you are preparing for the examination by "taking" an examination, not by reading extraneous and/or supererogatory textbooks.

In short, this PASSBOOK®, used directedly, should be an important factor in helping you to pass your test.

NONTRADITIONAL EDUCATION

Students returning to school as adults bring more varied experience to their studies than do the teenagers who begin college shortly after graduating from high school. As a result, there are numerous programs for students with nontraditional learning curves. Hundreds of colleges and universities grant degrees to people who cannot attend classes at a regular campus or have already learned what the college is supposed to teach.

You can earn nontraditional education credits in many ways:
- Passing standardized exams
- Demonstrating knowledge gained through experience
- Completing campus-based coursework, and
- Taking courses off campus

Some methods of assessing learning for credit are objective, such as standardized tests. Others are more subjective, such as a review of life experiences.

With some help from four hypothetical characters – Alice, Vin, Lynette, and Jorge – this article describes nontraditional ways of earning educational credit. It begins by describing programs in which you can earn a high school diploma without spending 4 years in a classroom. The college picture is more complicated, so it is presented in two parts: one on gaining credit for what you know through course work or experience, and a second on college degree programs. The final section lists resources for locating more information.

Earning High School Credit

People who were prevented from finishing high school as teenagers have several options if they want to do so as adults. Some major cities have back-to-school programs that allow adults to attend high school classes with current students. But the more practical alternatives for most adults are to take the General Educational Development (GED) tests or to earn a high school diploma by demonstrating their skills or taking correspondence classes.

Of course, these options do not match the experience of staying in high school and graduating with one's friends. But they are viable alternatives for adult learners committed to meeting and, often, continuing their educational goals.

GED Program

Alice quit high school her sophomore year and took a job to help support herself, her younger brother, and their newly widowed mother. Now an adult, she wants to earn her high school diploma – and then go on to college. Because her job as head cook and her family responsibilities keep her busy during the day, she plans to get a high school equivalency diploma. She will study for, and take, the GED tests. Every year, about half a million adults earn their high school credentials this way. A GED diploma is accepted in lieu of a high school one by more than 90 percent of employers, colleges, and universities, so it is a good choice for someone like Alice.

The GED testing program is sponsored by the American Council on Education and State and local education departments. It consists of examinations in five subject areas: Writing, science, mathematics, social studies, and literature and the arts. The tests also measure skills such as analytical ability, problem solving, reading comprehension, and ability to understand and apply information. Most of the questions are multiple choice; the writing test includes an essay section on a topic of general interest.

Eligibility rules for taking the exams vary, but some states require that you must be at least 18. Tests are given in English, Spanish, and French. In addition to standard print, versions in large print, Braille, and audiocassette are also available. Total time allotted for the tests is 7 1/2 hours.

The GED tests are not easy. About one-fourth of those who complete the exams every year do not pass. Passing scores are established by administering the tests to a sample of graduating high school seniors. The minimum standard score is set so that about one-third of graduating seniors would not pass the tests if they took them.

Because of the difficulty of the tests, people need to prepare themselves to take them. Often, they start by taking the Official GED Practice Tests, usually available through a local adult education center. Centers are listed in your phone book's blue pages under "Adult Education," "Continuing Education," or "GED." Adult education centers also have information about GED preparation classes and self-study materials. Classes are generally arranged to accommodate adults' work schedules. National Learning Corporation publishes several study guides that aim to thoroughly prepare test-takers for the GED.

School districts, colleges, adult education centers, and community organizations have information about GED testing schedules and practice tests. For more information, contact them, your nearest GED testing center, or:

GED Testing Service
One Dupont Circle, NW, Suite 250
Washington, DC 20036-1163
1(800) 62-MY GED (626-9433)
(202) 939-9490

Skills Demonstration

Adults who have acquired high school level skills through experience might be eligible for the National External Diploma Program. This alternative to the GED does not involve any direct instruction. Instead, adults seeking a high school diploma must demonstrate mastery of 65 competencies in 8 general areas: Communication; computation; occupational preparedness; and self, social, consumer, scientific, and technological awareness.

Mastery is shown through the completion of the tasks. For example, a participant could prove competency in computation by measuring a room for carpeting, figuring out the amount of carpet needed, and computing the cost.

Before being accepted for the program, adults undergo an evaluation. Tests taken at one of the program's offices measure reading, writing, and mathematics abilities. A take-home segment includes a self-assessment of current skills, an individual skill evaluation, and an occupational interest and aptitude test.

Adults accepted for the program have weekly meetings with an assessor. At the meeting, the assessor reviews the participant's work from the previous week. If the task has not been completed properly, the assessor explains the mistake. Participants continue to correct their errors until they master each competency. A high school diploma is awarded upon proven mastery of all 65 competencies.

Fourteen States and the District of Columbia now offer the External Diploma Program. For more information, contact:

External Diploma Program
One Dupont Circle, NW, Suite 250
Washington, DC 20036-1193
(202) 939-9475

Correspondence and Distance Study

Vin dropped out of high school during his junior year because his family's frequent moves made it difficult for him to continue his studies. He promised himself at the time he dropped out that he would someday finish the courses needed for his diploma. For people like Vin, who prefer to earn a traditional diploma in a nontraditional way, there are about a dozen accredited courses of study for earning a high school diploma by correspondence, or distance study. The programs are either privately run, affiliated with a university, or administered by a State education department.

Distance study diploma programs have no residency requirements, allowing students to continue their studies from almost any location. Depending on the course of study, students need not be enrolled full time and usually have more flexible schedules for finishing their work. Selection of courses ranges from vo-tech to college prep, and some programs place different emphasis on the types of diplomas offered. University affiliated schools, for example, allow qualified students to take college courses along with their high school ones. Students can then apply the college credits toward a degree at that university or transfer them to another institution.

Taking courses by distance study is often more challenging and time consuming than attending classes, especially for adults who have other obligations. Success depends on each student's motivation. Students usually do reading assignments on their own. Written exercises, which they complete and send to an instructor for grading, supplement their reading material.

A list of some accredited high schools that offer diplomas by distance study is available free from the Distance Education and Training Council, formerly known as the National Home Study Council. Request the "DETC Directory of Accredited Institutions" from:

The Distance Education and Training Council
1601 18th Street, NW.
Washington, DC 20009-2529
(202) 234-5100

Some publications profiling nontraditional college programs include addresses and descriptions of several high school correspondence ones. See the Resources section at the end of this article for more information.

Getting College Credit For What You Know

Adults can receive college credit for prior coursework, by passing examinations, and documenting experiential learning. With help from a college advisor, nontraditional students should assess their skills, establish their educational goals, and determine the number of college credits they might be eligible for.

Even before you meet with a college advisor, you should collect all your school and training records. Then, make a list of all knowledge and abilities acquired through experience, no matter how irrelevant they seem to your chosen field. Next, determine your educational goals: What specific field do you wish to study? What kind of a degree do you want? Finally, determine how your past work fits into the field of study. Later on, you will evaluate educational programs to find one that's right for you.

People who have complex educational or experiential learning histories might want to have their learning evaluated by the Regents Credit Bank. The Credit Bank, operated by Regents College of the University of the State of New York, allows people to consolidate credits earned through college, experience, or other methods. Special assessments are available for Regents College enrollees whose knowledge in a specific field cannot be adequately evaluated by standardized exams. For more information, contact the Regents Credit Bank at:

Regents College
7 Columbia Circle
Albany, NY 12203-5159
(518) 464-8500

Credit For Prior College Coursework

When Lynette was in college during the 1970s, she attended several different schools and took a variety of courses. She did well in some classes and poorly in others. Now that she is a successful business owner and has more focus, Lynette thinks she should forget about her previous coursework and start from scratch. Instead, she should start from where she is.

Lynette should have all her transcripts sent to the colleges or universities of her choice and let an admissions officer determine which classes are applicable toward a degree. A few credits here and there may not seem like much, but they add up. Even if the subjects do not seem relevant to any major, they might be counted as elective credits toward a degree. And comparing the cost of transcripts with the cost of college courses, it makes sense to spend a few dollars per transcript for a chance to save hundreds, and perhaps thousands, of dollars in books and tuition.

Rules for transferring credits apply to all prior coursework at accredited colleges and universities, whether done on campus or off. Courses completed off campus, often called extended learning, include those available to students through independent study and correspondence. Many schools have extended learning programs; Brigham Young University, for example, offers more than 300 courses through its Department of Independent Study. One type of extended learning is distance learning, a form of correspondence study by technological means such as television, video and audio, CD-ROM, electronic mail, and computer tutorials. See the Resources section at the end of this article for more information about publications available from the National University Continuing Education Association.

Any previously earned college credits should be considered for transfer, no matter what the subject or the grade received. Many schools do not accept the transfer of courses graded below a C or ones taken more than a designated number of years ago. Some colleges and universities also have limits on the number of credits that can be transferred and applied toward a degree. But not all do. For example, Thomas Edison State College, New Jersey's State college for adults, accepts the transfer of all 120 hours of credit required for a baccalaureate degree – provided all the credits are transferred from regionally accredited schools, no more than 80 are at the junior college level, and the student's grades overall and in the field of study average out to C.

To assign credit for prior coursework, most schools require original transcripts. This means you must complete a form or send a written, signed request to have your transcripts released directly to a college or university. Once you have chosen the schools you want to apply to, contact the schools you attended before. Find out how much each transcript costs, and ask them to send your transcripts to the ones you are applying to. Write a letter that includes your name (and names used during attendance, if different) and dates of attendance, along with the names and addresses of the schools to which your transcripts should be sent. Include payment and mail to the registrar at the schools you have attended. The registrar's office will process your request and send an official transcript of your coursework to the colleges or universities you have designated.

Credit For Noncollege Courses

Colleges and universities are not the only ones that offer classes. Volunteer organizations and employers often provide formal training worth college credit. The American Council on Education has two programs that assess thousands of specific courses and make recommendations on the amount of college credit they are worth. Colleges and universities accept the recommendations or use them as guidelines.

One program evaluates educational courses sponsored by government agencies, business and industry, labor unions, and professional and voluntary organizations. It is the Program on Noncollegiate Sponsored Instruction (PONSI). Some of the training seminars Alice has participated in covered topics such as food preparation, kitchen safety, and nutrition. Although she has not yet earned her GED, Alice can earn college credit because of her completion of these formal job-training seminars. The number of credits each seminar is worth does not hinge on Alice's current eligibility for college enrollment.

The other program evaluates courses offered by the Army, Navy, Air Force, Marines, Coast Guard, and Department of Defense. It is the Military Evaluations Program. Jorge has never attended college, but the engineering technology classes he completed as part of his military training are worth college credit. And as an Army veteran, Jorge is eligible for a service that takes the evaluations one step further. The Army/American Council on Education Registry Transcript System (AARTS) will provide Jorge with an individualized transcript of American Council on Education credit recommendations for all courses he completed, the military occupational specialties (MOS's) he held, and examinations he passed while in the Army. All Army and National Guard enlisted personnel and veterans who enlisted after October 1981 are eligible for the transcript. Similar services are being considered by the Navy and Marine Corps.

To obtain a free transcript, see your Army Education Center for a 5454R transcript request form. Include your name, Social Security number, basic active service date, and complete address where you want the transcript sent. Mail your request to:

AARTS Operations Center
415 McPherson Ave.
Fort Leavenworth, KS 66027-1373

Recommendations for PONSI are published in *The National Guide to Educational Credit for Training Programs;* military program recommendations are in *The Guide to the Evaluation of Educational Experiences in the Armed Forces.* See the Resources section at the end of this article for more information about these publications.

Former military personnel who took a foreign language course through the Defense Language Institute may request course transcripts by sending their name, Social Security number, course title, duration of the course, and graduation date to:
Commandant, Defense Language Institute
Attn: ATFL-DAA-AR
Transcripts
Presidio of Monterey
Monterey, CA 93944-5006

Not all of Jorge's and Alice's courses have been assessed by the American Council on Education. Training courses that have no Council credit recommendation should still be assessed by an advisor at the schools they want to attend. Course descriptions, class notes, test scores, and other documentation may be helpful for comparing training courses to their college equivalents. An oral examination or other demonstration of competency might also be required.

There is no guarantee you will receive all the credits you are seeking – but you certainly won't if you make no attempt.

Credit By Examination

Standardized tests are the best-known method of receiving college credit without taking courses. These exams are often taken by high school students seeking advanced placement for college, but they are also available to adult learners. Testing programs and colleges and universities offer exams in a number of subjects. Two U.S. Government institutes have foreign language exams for employees that also may be worth college credit.

It is important to understand that receiving a passing score on these exams does not mean you get college credit automatically. Each school determines which test results it will accept, minimum scores required, how scores are converted for credit, and the amount of credit, if any, to be assigned. Most colleges and universities accept the American Council on Education credit recommendations, published every other year in the 250-page *Guide to Educational Credit by Examination*. For more information, contact:
The American Council on Education
Credit by Examination Program
One Dupont Circle, Suite 250
Washington, DC 20036-1193
(202) 939-9434

Testing programs:

You might know some of the five national testing programs by their acronyms or initials: CLEP, ACT PEP: RCE, DANTES, AP, and NOCTI. (The meanings of these initialisms are explained below.) There is some overlap among programs; for example, four of them have introductory accounting exams. Since you will not be awarded credit more than once for a specific subject, you should carefully evaluate each program for the subject exams you wish to take. And before taking an exam, make sure you will be awarded credit by the college or university you plan to attend.

CLEP (College-Level Examination Program), administered by the College Board, is the most widely accepted of the national testing programs; more than 2,800 accredited schools award credit for passing exam scores. Each test covers material taught in basic undergraduate courses. There are five general exams – English composition, humanities, college mathematics, natural sciences, and social sciences and history – and many subject exams. Most exams are entirely multiple-choice, but English composition exams may include an essay section. For more information, contact:

    CLEP
    P.O. Box 6600
    Princeton, NJ 08541-6600
    (609) 771-7865

ACT PEP: RCE (American College Testing Proficiency Exam Program: Regents College Examinations) tests are given in 38 subjects within arts and sciences, business, education, and nursing. Each exam is recommended for either lower- or upper-level credit. Exams contain either objective or extended response questions, and are graded according to a standard score, letter grade, or pass/fail. Fees vary, depending on the subject and type of exam. For more information or to request free study guides, contact:

    ACT PEP: Regents College Examinations
    P.O. Box 4014
    Iowa City, IA 52243
    (319) 337-1387
    (New York State residents must contact Regents College directly.)

DANTES (Defense Activity for Nontraditional Education Support) standardized tests are developed by the Educational Testing Service for the Department of Defense. Originally administered only to military personnel, the exams have been available to the public since 1983. About 50 subject tests cover business, mathematics, social science, physical science, humanities, foreign languages, and applied technology. Most of the tests consist entirely of multiple-choice questions. Schools determine their own administering fees and testing schedules. For more information or to request free study sheets, contact:

    DANTES Program Office
    Mail Stop 31-X
    Educational Testing Service
    Princeton, NJ 08541
    1(800) 257-9484

The AP (Advanced Placement) Program is a cooperative effort between secondary schools and colleges and universities. AP exams are developed each year by committees of college and high school faculty appointed by the College Board and assisted by consultants from the Educational Testing Service. Subjects include arts and languages, natural sciences, computer science, social sciences, history, and mathematics. Most tests are 2 or 3 hours long and include both multiple-choice and essay questions. AP courses are available to help students prepare for exams, which are offered in the spring. For more information about the Advanced Placement Program, contact:

    Advanced Placement Services
    P.O. Box 6671
    Princeton, NJ 08541-6671
    (609) 771-7300

NOCTI (National Occupational Competency Testing Institute) assessments are designed for people like Alice, who have vocational-technical skills that cannot be evaluated by other tests. NOCTI assesses competency at two levels: Student/job ready and teacher/experienced worker. Standardized evaluations are available for occupations such as auto-body repair, electronics, mechanical drafting, quantity food preparation, and upholstering. The tests consist of multiple-choice questions and a performance component. Other services include workshops, customized assessments, and pre-testing. For more information, contact:

NOCTI
500 N. Bronson Ave.
Ferris State University
Big Rapids, MI 49307
(616) 796-4699

Colleges and universities:

Many colleges and universities have credit-by-exam programs, through which students earn credit by passing a comprehensive exam for a course offered by the institution. Among the most widely recognized are the programs at Ohio University, the University of North Carolina, Thomas Edison State College, and New York University.

Ohio University offers about 150 examinations for credit. In addition, you may sometimes arrange to take special examinations in non-laboratory courses offered at Ohio University. To take a test for credit, you must enroll in the course. If you plan to transfer the credit earned, you also need written permission from an official at your school. Books and study materials are available, for a cost, through the university. Exams must be taken within 6 months of the enrollment date; most last 3 hours. You may arrange to take the exam off campus if you do not live near the university.

Ohio University is on the quarter-hour system; most courses are worth 4 quarter hours, the equivalent of 3 semester hours. For more information, contact:

Independent Study
Tupper Hall 302
Ohio University
Athens, OH 45701-2979
1(800) 444-2910
(614) 593-2910

The University of North Carolina offers a credit-by-examination option for 140 independent study (correspondence) courses in foreign languages, humanities, social sciences, mathematics, business administration, education, electrical and computer engineering, health administration, and natural sciences. To take an exam, you must request and receive approval from both the course instructor and the independent studies department. Exams must be taken within six months of enrollment, and you may register for no more than two at a time. If you are not near the University's Chapel Hill campus, you may take your exam under supervision at an accredited college, university, community college, or technical institute. For more information, contact:

Independent Studies
CB #1020, The Friday Center
UNC-Chapel Hill
Chapel Hill, NC 27599-1020
1(800) 862-5669 / (919) 962-1134

The Thomas Edison College Examination Program offers more than 50 exams in liberal arts, business, and professional areas. Thomas Edison State College administers tests twice a month in Trenton, New Jersey; however, students may arrange to take their tests with a proctor at any accredited American college or university or U.S. military base. Most of the tests are multiple choice; some also include short answer or essay questions. Time limits range from 90 minutes to 4 hours, depending on the exam. For more information, contact:

    Thomas Edison State College
    TECEP, Office of Testing and Assessment
    101 W. State Street
    Trenton, NJ 08608-1176
    (609) 633-2844

New York University's Foreign Language Program offers proficiency exams in more than 40 languages, from Albanian to Yiddish. Two exams are available in each language: The 12-point test is equivalent to 4 undergraduate semesters, and the 16-point exam may lead to upper level credit. The tests are given at the university's Foreign Language Department throughout the year.

Proof of foreign language proficiency does not guarantee college credit. Some colleges and universities accept transcripts only for languages commonly taught, such as French and Spanish. Nontraditional programs are more likely than traditional ones to grant credit for proficiency in other languages.

For an informational brochure and registration form for NYU's foreign language proficiency exams, contact:

    New York University
    Foreign Language Department
    48 Cooper Square, Room 107
    New York, NY 10003
    (212) 998-7030

Government institutes:

The Defense Language Institute and Foreign Service Institute administer foreign language proficiency exams for personnel stationed abroad. Usually, the tests are given at the end of intensive language courses or upon completion of service overseas. But some people – like Jorge, who knows Spanish – speak another language fluently and may be allowed to take a proficiency exam in that language before completing their tour of duty. Contact one of the offices listed below to obtain transcripts of those scores. Proof of proficiency does not guarantee college credit, however, as discussed above.

To request score reports from the Defense Language Institute for Defense Language Proficiency Tests, send your name, Social Security number, language for which you were tested, and, most importantly, when and where you took the exam to:

    Commandant, Defense Language Institute
    Attn: ATFL-ES-T
    DLPT Score Report Request
    Presidio of Monterey
    Monterey, CA 93944-5006

To request transcripts of scores for Foreign Service Institute exams, send your name, Social Security number, language for which you were tested, and dates or year of exams to:

Foreign Service Institute
Arlington Hall
4020 Arlington Boulevard
Rosslyn, VA 22204-1500
Attn: Testing Office (Send your request to the attention of the testing office of the foreign language in which you were tested)

Credit For Experience

Experiential learning credit may be given for knowledge gained through job responsibilities, personal hobbies, volunteer opportunities, homemaking, and other experiences. Colleges and universities base credit awards on the knowledge you have attained, not for the experience alone. In addition, the knowledge must be college level; not just any learning will do. Throwing horseshoes as a hobby is not likely to be worth college credit. But if you've done research on how and where the sport originated, visited blacksmiths, organized tournaments, and written a column for a trade journal – well, that's a horseshoe of a different color.

Adults attempting to get credit for their experience should be forewarned: Having your experience evaluated for college credit is time-consuming, tedious work – not an easy shortcut for people who want quick-fix college credits. And not all experience, no matter how valuable, is the equivalent of college courses.

Requesting college credit for your experiential learning can be tricky. You should get assistance from a credit evaluations officer at the school you plan to attend, but you should also have a general idea of what your knowledge is worth. A common method for converting knowledge into credit is to use a college catalog. Find course titles and descriptions that match what you have learned through experience, and request the number of credits offered for those courses.

Once you know what credit to ask for, you must usually present your case in writing to officials at the college you plan to attend. The most common form of presenting experiential learning for credit is the portfolio. A portfolio is a written record of your knowledge along with a request for equivalent college credit. It includes an identification and description of the knowledge for which you are requesting credit, an explanatory essay of how the knowledge was gained and how it fits into your educational plans, documentation that you have acquired such knowledge, and a request for college credit. Required elements of a portfolio vary by schools but generally follow those guidelines.

In identifying knowledge you have gained, be specific about exactly what you have learned. For example, it is not enough for Lynette to say she runs a business. She must identify the knowledge she has gained from running it, such as personnel management, tax law, marketing strategy, and inventory review. She must also include brief descriptions about her knowledge of each to support her claims of having those skills.

The essay gives you a chance to relay something about who you are. It should address your educational goals, include relevant autobiographical details, and be well organized, neat, and convey confidence. In his essay, Jorge might first state his goal of becoming an engineer. Then he would explain why he joined the Army, where he got hands-on training and experience in developing and servicing electronic equipment.

This, he would say, led to his hobby of creating remote-controlled model cars, of which he has built 20. His conclusion would highlight his accomplishments and tie them to his desire to become an electronic engineer.

Documentation is evidence that you've learned what you claim to have learned. You can show proof of knowledge in a variety of ways, including audio or video recordings, letters from current or former employers describing your specific duties and job performance, blueprints, photographs or artwork, and transcripts of certifying exams for professional licenses and certification – such as Alice's certification from the American Culinary Federation. Although documentation can take many forms, written proof alone is not always enough. If it is impossible to document your knowledge in writing, find out if your experiential learning can be assessed through supplemental oral exams by a faculty expert.

Earning a College Degree

Nontraditional students often have work, family, and financial obligations that prevent them from quitting their jobs to attend school full time. Can they still meet their educational goals? Yes.

More than 150 accredited colleges and universities have nontraditional bachelor's degree programs that require students to spend little or no time on campus; over 300 others have nontraditional campus-based degree programs. Some of those schools, as well as most junior and community colleges, offer associate's degrees nontraditionally. Each school with a nontraditional course of study determines its own rules for awarding credit for prior coursework, exams, or experience, as discussed previously. Most have charges on top of tuition for providing these special services.

Several publications profile nontraditional degree programs; see the Resources section at the end of this article for more information. To determine which school best fits your academic profile and educational goals, first list your criteria. Then, evaluate nontraditional programs based on their accreditation, features, residency requirements, and expenses. Once you have chosen several schools to explore further, write to them for more information. Detailed explanations of school policies should help you decide which ones you want to apply to.

Get beyond the printed word – especially the glowing words each school writes about itself. Check out the schools you are considering with higher education authorities, alumni, employers, family members, and friends. If possible, visit the campus to talk to students and instructors and sit in on a few classes, even if you will be completing most or all of your work off campus. Ask school officials questions about such things as enrollment numbers, graduation rate, faculty qualifications, and confusing details about the application process or academic policies. After you have thoroughly investigated each prospective college or university, you can make an informed decision about which is right for you.

Accreditation

Accreditation is a process colleges and universities submit to voluntarily for getting their credentials. An accredited school has been investigated and visited by teams of observers and has periodic inspections by a private accrediting agency. The initial review can take two years or more.

Regional agencies accredit entire schools, and professional agencies accredit either specialized schools or departments within schools. Although there are no national accrediting standards, not just any accreditation will do. Countless "accreditation associations" have been invented by schools, many of which have no academic programs and sell phony degrees, to accredit themselves. But 6 regional and about 80 professional accrediting associations in the United States are recognized by the U.S. Department of Education or the Commission on Recognition of Postsecondary Accreditation. When checking accreditation, these are the names to look for. For more information about accreditation and accrediting agencies, contact:

    Institutional Participation Oversight Service Accreditation and State Liaison Division
    U.S. Department of Education
    ROB 3, Room 3915
    600 Independence Ave., SW
    Washington, DC 20202-5244
    (202) 708-7417

Because accreditation is not mandatory, lack of accreditation does not necessarily mean a school or program is bad. Some schools choose not to apply for accreditation, are in the process of applying, or have educational methods too unconventional for an accrediting association's standards. For the nontraditional student, however, earning a degree from a college or university with recognized accreditation is an especially important consideration. Although nontraditional education is becoming more widely accepted, it is not yet mainstream. Employers skeptical of a degree earned in a nontraditional manner are likely to be even less accepting of one from an unaccredited school.

Program Features

Because nontraditional students have diverse educational objectives, nontraditional schools are diverse in what they offer. Some programs are geared toward helping students organize their scattered educational credits to get a degree as quickly as possible. Others cater to those who may have specific credits or experience but need assistance in completing requirements. Whatever your educational profile, you should look for a program that works with you in obtaining your educational goals.

A few nontraditional programs have special admissions policies for adult learners like Alice, who plan to earn their GEDs but want to enroll in college in the meantime. Other features of nontraditional programs include individualized learning agreements, intensive academic counseling, cooperative learning and internship placement, and waiver of some prerequisites or other requirements – as well as college credit for prior coursework, examinations, and experiential learning, all discussed previously.

Lynette, whose primary goal is to finish her degree, wants to earn maximum credits for her business experience. She will look for programs that do not limit the number of credits awarded for equivalency exams and experiential learning. And since well-documented proof of knowledge is essential for earning experiential learning credits, Lynette should make sure the program she chooses provides assistance to students submitting a portfolio.

Jorge, on the other hand, has more credits than he needs in certain areas and is willing to forego some. To become an engineer, he must have a bachelor's degree; but because he is accustomed to hands-on learning, Jorge is interested in getting experience as he gains more technical skills. He will concentrate on finding schools with strong cooperative education, supervised fieldwork, or internship programs.

Residency Requirements

Programs are sometimes deemed nontraditional because of their residency requirements. Many people think of residency for colleges and universities in terms of tuition, with in-state students paying less than out-of-state ones. Residency also may refer to where a student lives, either on or off campus, while attending school.

But in nontraditional education, residency usually refers to how much time students must spend on campus, regardless of whether they attend classes there. In some nontraditional programs, students need not ever step foot on campus. Others require only a very short residency, such as one day or a few weeks. Many schools have standard residency requirements of several semesters but schedule classes for evenings or weekends to accommodate working adults.

Lynette, who previously took courses by independent study, prefers to earn credits by distance study. She will focus on schools that have no residency requirement. Several colleges and universities have nonresident degree completion programs for adults with some college credit. Under the direction of a faculty advisor, students devise a plan for earning their remaining credits. Methods for earning credits include independent study, distance learning, seminars, supervised fieldwork, and group study at arranged sites. Students may have to earn a certain number of credits through the degree-granting institution. But many programs allow students to take courses at accredited schools of their choice for transfer toward their degree.

Alice wants to attend lectures but has an unpredictable schedule. Her best course of action will be to seek out short residency programs that require students to attend seminars once or twice a semester. She can take courses that are televised and videotape them to watch when her schedule permits, with the seminars helping to ensure that she properly completes her coursework. Many colleges and universities with short residency requirements also permit students to earn some credits elsewhere, by whatever means the student chooses.

Some fields of study require classroom instruction. As Jorge will discover, few colleges and universities allow students to earn a bachelor's degree in engineering entirely through independent study. Nontraditional residency programs are designed to accommodate adults' daytime work schedules. Jorge should look for programs offering evening, weekend, summer, and accelerated courses.

Tuition and Other Expenses

The final decisions about which schools Alice, Jorge, and Lynette attend may hinge in large part on a single issue: Cost. And rising tuition is only part of the equation. Beginning with application fees and continuing through graduation fees, college expenses add up.

Traditional and nontraditional students have some expenses in common, such as the cost of books and other materials. Tuition might even be the same for some courses, especially for colleges and universities offering standard ones at unusual times. But for nontraditional programs, students may also pay fees for services such as credit or transcript review, evaluation, advisement, and portfolio assessment.

Students are also responsible for postage and handling or setup expenses for independent study courses, as well as for all examination and transcript fees for transferring credits. Usually, the more nontraditional the program, the more detailed the fees. Some schools charge a yearly enrollment fee rather than tuition for degree completion candidates who want their files to remain active.

Although tuition and fees might seem expensive, most educators tell you not to let money come between you and your educational goals. Talk to someone in the financial aid department of the school you plan to attend or check your library for publications about financial aid sources. The U.S. Department of Education publishes a guide to Federal aid programs such as Pell Grants, student loans, and work-study. To order the free 74-page booklet, *The Student Guide: Financial Aid from the U.S. Department of Education,* contact:

    Federal Student Aid Information Center
    P.O. Box 84
    Washington, DC 20044
    1 (800) 4FED-AID (433-3243)

Resources

Information on how to earn a high school diploma or college degree without following the usual routes is available from several organizations and in numerous publications. Information on nontraditional graduate degree programs, available for master's through doctoral level, though not discussed in this article, can usually be obtained from the same resources that detail bachelor's degree programs.

National Learning Corporation publishes study guides for all of these exams, for both general examinations and tests in specific subject areas. To order study guides, or to browse their catalog featuring more than 5,000 titles, visit NLC online at www.passbooks.com, or contact them by phone at (800) 632-8888.

Organizations

Adult learners should always contact their local school system, community college, or university to learn about programs that are readily available. The following national organizations can also supply information:

    American Council on Education
    One Dupont Circle
    Washington, DC 20036-1193
    (202) 939-9300

Within the American Council on Education, the Center for Adult Learning and Educational Credentials administers the National External Diploma Program, the GED Program, the Program on Noncollegiate Sponsored Instruction, the Credit by Examination Program, and the Military Evaluations Program.

DANTES Subject Standardized Tests

INTRODUCTION

The DANTES (Defense Activity for Non-Traditional Education Support) subject standardized tests are comprehensive college and graduate level examinations given by the Armed Forces, colleges and graduate schools as end-of-subject course evaluation final examinations or to obtain college equivalency credits in the various subject areas tested.

The DANTES Examination Program enables students to obtain college credit for what they have learned on the job, through self-study, personal interest, correspondence courses or by any other means. It is used by colleges and universities to award college credit to students who demonstrate that they know as much as students completing an equivalent college course. It is a cost-efficient, time-saving way for students to use their knowledge to accomplish their educational goals.

Most schools accept the American Council on Education (ACE) recommendations for the minimum score required and the amount of credit awarded, but not all schools do. Be sure to check the policy regarding the score level required for credit and the number of credits to be awarded.

Not all tests are accepted by all institutions. Even when a test is accepted by an institution, it may not be acceptable for every program at that institution. Before considering testing, ascertain the acceptability of a specific test for a particular course.

Colleges and universities that administer DANTES tests may administer them to any applicant – or they may administer the tests only to students registered at their institution. Decisions about who will be allowed to test are made by the school. Students should contact the test center to determine current policies and schedules for DANTES testing.

Colleges and universities authorized to administer DANTES tests usually do so throughout the calendar year. Each school sets its own fee for test administration and establishes its own testing schedule. Contact the representative at the administering school directly to make arrangements for testing.

Checklist
For Students

- ✓ Visit **www.getcollegecredit.com** to obtain a list of tests, fact sheets, test preparation materials, participating colleges and universities, and much more.

- ✓ Contact your school advisor to confirm that the DSST you selected will fit into your curriculum.

- ✓ Consult the ***DSST Candidate Information Bulletin*** for answers to specific questions.

- ✓ Contact the test site to schedule your test.

- ✓ Prepare for your examination by using the fact sheet as a guide.

- ✓ Take the test.

If you would like a score report sent to your college or university, it is a good idea to bring the four-digit code with you. You must write the DSST Test Center Code for that institution on your answer sheet at the time of testing. DSST Test Center Codes are noted in the DSST Participating Colleges and Universities listing on the Web site.

If you prefer to send a score report to an institution at a later date, there is a transcript fee of $20 for each transcript ordered.

Thomson Prometric
DSST Program
2000 Lenox Drive, Third Floor
Lawrenceville, NJ 08648

Toll-free: 877-471-9860
609-895-5011

E-mail: pnj-dsst@thomson.com

MAKING A COLLEGE DEGREE WITHIN YOUR REACH

Today, there are many educational alternatives to the classroom—you can learn from your job, your reading, your independent study, and special interests you pursue. You may already have learned the subject matter covered by some college-level courses.

The DSST Program is a nationally recognized testing program that gives you the opportunity to receive college credit for learning acquired outside the traditional college classroom. Colleges and universities throughout the United States administer the program, developed by Thomson Prometric, year-round. Annually, over 90,000 DSSTs are administered to individuals who are interested in continuing their education. Take advantage of the DSST testing program; it speeds the educational process and provides the flexibility adults need, making earning a degree more feasible.

Since requirements differ from college to college, please check with the credit-awarding institution before taking a DSST. More than 1,800 colleges and universities currently award credit for DSSTs, and the number is growing every day. You can choose from 37 test titles in the areas of Social Science, Business, Mathematics, Applied Technology, Humanities, and Physical Science. A brief description of each examination is found on the pages that follow.

Reach Your Career Goals Through DSSTs

Use DSSTs to help you earn your degree, get a promotion, or simply demonstrate that you have college-level knowledge in subjects relevant to your work.

Save Time...

You don't have to sit through classes when you have previously acquired the knowledge or experience for most of what is being taught and can learn the rest yourself. You might be able to bypass introductory-level courses in subject areas you already know.

Save Money...

DSSTs save you money because the classes you bypass by earning credit through the DSST Program are classes you won't have to pay for on your way to earning your degree. You can use the money instead to take more advanced courses that can be more challenging and rewarding.

Improve Your Chances for Admission to College

Each college has its own admission policies; however, having passing scores for DSSTs on your transcript can provide strong evidence of how well you can perform at the college level.

Gain Confidence Performing at a College Level

Many adults returning to college find that lack of confidence is often the greatest hurdle to overcome. Passing a DSST demonstrates your ability to perform on a college level.

Make Up for Courses You May Have Missed

You may be ready to graduate from college and find that you are a few credits short of earning your degree. By using semester breaks, vacation time, or leisure time to study independently, you can prepare to take one or more DSSTs, fulfill your academic requirements, and graduate on time.

If You Cannot Attend Regularly Scheduled Classes...

If your lifestyle or responsibilities prevent you from attending regularly scheduled classes, you can earn your college degree from a college offering an external degree program. The DSST Program allows you to earn your degree by study and experience outside the traditional classroom.

Many colleges and universities offer external degree or distance learning programs. For additional information, contact the college you plan to attend or:

Center for Lifelong Learning
American Council on Education
One DuPont Circle NW, Suite 250
Washington, DC 20036
202-939-9475
www.acenet.edu
(Select "Center for Lifelong Learning" under "Programs & Services"
for more information)

Fact Sheets

For each test, there is a Fact Sheet that outlines the topics covered by each test and includes a list of sample questions, a list of recommended references of books that would be useful for review, and the number of credits awarded for a passing score as recommended by the American Council on Education (ACE). *Please note that some schools require scores that are higher than the minimum ACE-recommended passing score.* It is suggested that you check with your college or university to determine what score they require in order to earn credit. You can obtain Fact Sheets by:
- Downloading them from www.getcollegecredit.com
- E-mailing a request to pnj-dsst@thomson.com
- Completing a Candidate Publications Order Form

DSST Online Practice Tests

DSST online practice tests contain items that reflect a *partial range of difficulty* identified in the Content Outline section on each Fact Sheet. There is an online DSST Practice Test in the following categories:
- Mathematics
- Social Science
- Business
- Physical Science
- Applied Technology
- Humanities

Although the online DSST Practice Test questions do not indicate the full range of difficulty you would find in an actual DSST test, they will help you assess your knowledge level. Each online DSST Practice Test can be purchased by visiting www.getcollegecredit.com and clicking on DSST Practice Exams.

TAKING DSST EXAMINATIONS

Earning College Credit for DSST Examinations

To find out if the college of your choice awards credit for passing DSST scores, contact the admissions office or counseling and testing office. The college can also provide information on the scores required for awarding credit, the number of credit hours awarded, and any courses that can be bypassed with satisfactory scores.

It is important that you contact the institution of your choice as early as possible since credit-awarding policies differ among colleges and universities.

Where to Take DSSTs

DSSTs are administered at colleges and universities nationwide. Each location determines the frequency and scheduling of test administrations. To obtain the most current list of participating DSST colleges and universities:
- Visit and download the information from www.getcollegecredit.com
- E-mail pnj-dsst@thomson.com

Scheduling Your Examination

Please be aware that some colleges and universities provide DSST testing services to enrolled students only. After you have selected a college or university that administers DSSTs, you will need to contact them to schedule your test date.

The fee to take a DSST is $60 per test. This fee entitles you to two score reports after the test is scored. One will be sent directly to you and the other will be sent to the college or university that you designate on your answer sheet. You may pay the test fee with a certified check or U.S. money order made payable to Thomson Prometric or you may charge the test fee to your Visa, MasterCard or American Express credit card. Note: The credit card statement will reflect a charge from Thomson Prometric for all DSST examinations. *(Declined credit card charges will be assessed an additional $25 processing fee.)*

In addition, the test site may also require a test administration fee for each examination, to be paid directly to the institution. Contact the test site to determine its administration fee and payment policy.

Other Testing Arrangements

If you are unable to find a participating DSST college or university in your area, you may want to contact the testing office of a local accredited college or university to determine whether a representative from that office will agree to administer the test(s) for you.

The school's representative should then contact the DSST Program at 866-794-3497 to arrange for this administration. If you are unable to locate a test site, contact Thomson Prometric for assistance at pnj-dsst@thomson.com or 866-794-3497.

Testing Accommodations for Students with Disabilities

Thomson Prometric is committed to serving test takers with disabilities by providing services and reasonable testing accommodations as set forth in the provisions of the *Americans with Disabilities Act* (ADA). If you have a disability, as prescribed by the ADA, and require special testing services or arrangements, please contact the test administrator at the test site. You will be asked to submit to the test administrator documentation of your disability and your request for special accommodations. The test administrator will then forward your documentation along with your request for testing accommodations to Thomson Prometric for approval.

Please submit your request as far in advance of your test date as possible so that the necessary accommodations can be made. Only test takers with documented disabilities are eligible for special accommodations.

On the Day of the Examination

It is important to review this information and to have the correct identification present on the day of the examination:
- Arrive on time as a courtesy to the test administrator.
- Bring a valid form of government-issued identification that includes a current photo and your signature (acceptable documents include a driver's license, passport, state-issued identification card or military identification). *Anyone who fails to present valid identification will not be allowed to test.*
- Bring several No. 2 (soft-lead) sharpened pencils with good erasers, a watch, and a black pen if you will be writing an essay.
- Do not bring books or papers.
- Do not bring an alarm watch that beeps, a telephone, or a phone beeper into the testing room.
- The use of nonprogrammable calculators, slide rules, scratch paper and/or other materials is permitted for some of the tests.

DSST SCORING POLICIES

Your DSST examination scores are reported only to you, unless you request that they be sent elsewhere. If you want your scores sent to your college, you must provide the correct DSST code number of the school on your answer sheet at the time you take the test. See the *DSST Directory of Colleges and Universities* on the Web site www.getcollegecredit.com.

If your institution is not listed, contact Thomson Prometric at 866-794-3497 to establish a code number. (Some schools may require a student to be enrolled prior to receiving a score report.)

Receiving Your Score Report

Allow approximately four weeks after testing to receive your score report.

Calling DSST Customer Service before the required four-week score processing time has elapsed will not expedite the processing of your scores. Due to privacy and security requirements, scores will not be reported to students over the telephone under any circumstance.

Scoring of Principles of Public Speaking Speeches

The speech portion of the *Principles of Public Speaking* examination will be sent to speech raters who are faculty members at accredited colleges that currently teach or have previously taught the course. Scores for the *Principles of Public Speaking* examination are available six to eight weeks from receipt by Thomson Prometric. If you take the *Principles of Public Speaking* examination and fail (either the objective, speech portion, or both), you must follow the retesting policy waiting period of six months (180 days) before retaking the entire exam.

Essays

The essays for *Ethics in America* and *Technical Writing* are optional and thus are not scored by raters. The essays are forwarded to the college or university that you designate, along with your score report, for their use in determining the award of credit. Before taking the *Ethics in America* or *Technical Writing* examinations, check with your college or university to determine whether the essay is required.

NOTE: *Principles of Public Speaking* speech topic cassette tapes and essays are kept on file at Thomson Prometric for one year from the date of administration.

How to Get Transcripts

There is a $20 fee for each transcript you request. Payment must be in the form of a certified check, U.S. money order payable to Thomson Prometric, or credit card. Personal checks and debit cards are NOT an acceptable method of payment. One transcript may include scores for one or more examinations taken. To request a transcript, download the Transcript Order Form from www.getcollegecredit.com.

DESCRIPTION OF THE DSST EXAMINATIONS

Mathematics

- **Fundamentals of College Algebra** covers mathematical concepts such as fundamental algebraic operations; linear, absolute value; quadratic equations, inequalities, radials, exponents and logarithms, factoring polynomials and graphing. The use of a nonprogrammable, handheld calculator is permitted.

- **Principles of Statistics** tests the understanding of the various topics of statistics, both qualitatively and quantitatively, and the ability to apply statistical methods to solve a variety of problems. The topics included in this test are descriptive statistics; correlation and regression; probability; chance models and sampling and tests of significance. The use of a nonprogrammable, handheld calculator is permitted.

Social Science

- **Art of the Western World** deals with the history of art during the following periods: classical; Romanesque and Gothic; early Renaissance; high Renaissance, Baroque; rococo; neoclassicism and romanticism; realism, impressionism and post-impressionism; early twentieth century; and post-World War II.

- **Western Europe Since 1945** tests the knowledge of basic facts and terms and the understanding of concepts and principles related to the areas of the historical background of the aftermath of the Second World War and rebuilding of Europe; national political systems; issues and policies in Western European societies; European institutions and processes; and Europe's relations with the rest of the world.

- **An Introduction to the Modern Middle East** emphasizes core knowledge (including geography, Judaism, Christianity, Islam, ethnicity); nineteenth-century European impact; twentieth-century Western influences; World Wars I and II; new nations; social and cultural changes (1900-1960) and the Middle East from 1960 to present.

- **Human/Cultural Geography** includes the Earth and basic facts (coordinate systems, maps, physiography, atmosphere, soils and vegetation, water); culture and environment, spatial processes (social processes, modern economic systems, settlement patterns, political geography); and regional geography.

- **Rise and Fall of the Soviet Union** covers Russia under the Old Regime; the Revolutionary Period; New Economic Policy; Pre-war Stalinism; The Second World War; Post-war Stalinism; The Khrushchev Years; The Brezhnev Era; and reform and collapse.

- **A History of the Vietnam War** covers the history of the roots of the Vietnam War; the First Vietnam War (1946-1954); pre-war developments (1954-1963); American involvement in the Vietnam War; Tet (1968); Vietnamizing the War (1968-1973); Cambodia and Laos; peace; legacies and lessons.

- **The Civil War and Reconstruction** covers the Civil War from presecession (1861) through Reconstruction. It includes causes of the war; secession; Fort Sumter; the war in the east and in the west; major battles; the political situation; assassination of Lincoln; end of the Confederacy; and Reconstruction.

- **Foundations of Education** includes topics such as contemporary issues in education; past and current influences on education (philosophies, democratic ideals, social/economic influences); and the interrelationships between contemporary issues and influences.

- **Life-span Developmental Psychology** covers models and theories; methods of study; ethical issues; biological development; perception, learning and memory; cognition and language; social, emotional, and personality development; social behaviors, family life cycle, extrafamilial settings; singlehood and cohabitation; occupational development and retirement; adjustment to life stresses; and bereavement and loss.

- **Drug and Alcohol Abuse** includes such topics as drug use in society; classification of drugs; pharmacological principles; alcohol (types, effects of, alcoholism); general principles and use of sedative hypnotics, narcotic analgesics, stimulants, and hallucinogens; other drugs (inhalants, steroids); and prevention/treatment.

- **General Anthropology** deals with anthropology as a discipline; theoretical perspectives; physical anthropology; archaeology; social organization; economic organization; political organization; religion; and modernization and application of anthropology.

- **Introduction to Law Enforcement** includes topics such as history and professional movement of law enforcement; overview of the U.S. criminal justice system; police systems in the U.S.; police organization, management, and issues; and U.S. law and precedents.

- **Criminal Justice** deals with criminal behavior (crime in the U.S., theories of crime, types of crime); the criminal justice system (historical origins, legal foundations, due process); police; the court system (history and organization, adult court system, juvenile court, pre-trial and post-trial processes); and corrections.

- **Fundamentals of Counseling** covers historical development (significant influences and people); counselor roles and functions; the counseling relationship; and theoretical approaches to counseling.

Business
- **Principles of Finance** deals with financial statements and planning; time value of money; working capital management; valuation and characteristics; capital budgeting; cost of capital; risk and return; and international financial management. The use of a nonprogrammable, handheld calculator is permitted.

- **Principles of Financial Accounting** includes topics such as general concepts and principles, accounting cycle and classification; transaction analysis; accruals and deferrals; cash and internal control; current accounts; long- and short-term liabilities; capital stock; and financial statements. The use of a nonprogrammable, handheld calculator is permitted.

- **Human Resource Management** covers general employment issues; job analysis; training and development; performance appraisals; compensation issues; security issues; personnel legislation and regulation; labor relations and current issues; an overview of the Human Resource Management Field; Human Resource Planning; Staffing; training and development; compensation issues; safety and health; employee rights and discipline; employment law; labor relations and current issues and trends.

- **Organizational Behavior** deals with the study of organizational behavior (scientific approaches, research designs, data collection methods); individual processes and characteristics; interpersonal and group processes and characteristics; organizational processes and characteristics; and change and development processes.

- **Principles of Supervision** deals with the roles and responsibilities of the supervisor; management functions (planning, organization and staffing, directing at the supervisory level); and other topics (legal issues, stress management, union environments, quality concerns).

- **Business Law II** covers topics such as sales of goods; debtor and creditor relations; business organizations; property; and commercial paper.

- **Introduction to Computing** includes topics such as history and technological generations; hardware/software; applications to information technology; program development; data management; communications and connectivity; and computing and society. The use of a nonprogrammable, handheld calculator is permitted.

- **Management Information Systems** covers systems theory, analysis and design of systems, hardware and software; database management; telecommunications; management of the MIS functional area and informational support.

- **Introduction to Business** deals with economic issues affecting business; international business; government and business; forms of business ownership; small business, entrepreneurship and franchise; management process; human resource management; production and operations; marketing management; financial management; risk management and insurance; and management and information systems.

- **Money and Banking** covers the role and kinds of money; commercial banks and other financial intermediaries; central banking and the Federal Reserve system; money and macroeconomics activity; monetary policy in the U.S.; and the international monetary system.

- **Personal Finance** includes topics such as financial goals and values; budgeting; credit and debt; major purchases; taxes; insurance; investments; and retirement and estate planning. The use of auxiliary materials, such as calculators and slide rules, is NOT permitted.

- **Business Mathematics** deals with basic operations with integers, fractions, and decimals; round numbers; ratios; averages; business graphs; simple interest; compound interest and annuities; net pay and deductions; discounts and markups; depreciation and net worth; corporate securities; distribution of ownership; and stock and asset turnover.

Physical Science
• **Astronomy** covers the history of astronomy, celestial mechanics; celestial systems; astronomical instruments; the solar system; nature and evolution; the galaxy; the universe; determining astronomical distances; and life in the universe.

• **Here's to Your Health** covers mental health and behavior; human development and relationships; substance abuse; fitness and nutrition; risk factors, disease, and disease prevention; and safety, consumer awareness, and environmental concerns.

• **Environment and Humanity** deals with topics such as ecological concepts (ecosystems, global ecology, food chains and webs); environmental impacts; environmental management and conservation; and political processes and the future.

• **Principles of Physical Science I** includes physics: Newton's Laws of Motion; energy and momentum; thermodynamics; wave and optics; electricity and magnetism; chemistry: properties of matter; atomic theory and structure; and chemical reactions.

• **Physical Geology** covers Earth materials; igneous, sedimentary, and metamorphic rocks; surface processes (weathering, groundwater, glaciers, oceanic systems, deserts and winds, hydrologic cycle); internal Earth processes; and applications (mineral and energy resources, environmental geology).

Applied Technology
• **Technical Writing** covers topics such as theory and practice of technical writing; purpose, content, and organizational patterns of common types of technical documents; elements of various technical reports; and technical editing. Students have the option to write a short essay on one of the technical topics provided. Thomson Prometric will not score the essay; however, for determining the award of credit, a copy of the essay will be forwarded to the college or university you've designated along with the score report or transcript.

Humanities
• **Ethics in America** deals with ethical traditions (Greek views, Biblical traditions, moral law, consequential ethics, feminist ethics); ethical analysis of issues arising in interpersonal and personal-societal relationships and in professional and occupational roles; and relationships between ethical traditions and the ethical analysis of situations. Students have the option to write an essay to analyze a morally problematic situation in terms of issues relevant to a decision and arguments for alternative positions. Thomson Prometric will not score the essay; however, for determining the award of credit, a copy of the essay will be forwarded to the college or university you've designated along with the score report or transcript.

• **Introduction to World Religions** covers topics such as dimensions and approaches to religion; primal religions; Hinduism; Buddhism; Confucianism; Taoism; Judaism; Christianity; and Islam.

• **Principles of Public Speaking** consists of two parts: Part One consists of multiple-choice questions covering considerations of Principles of Public Speaking; audience analysis; purposes of speeches; structure/organization; content/supporting materials; research; language and style; delivery; communication apprehension; listening and feedback; and criticism and evaluation. Part Two requires the student to record an impromptu persuasive speech that will be scored.

FREQUENTLY ASKED QUESTIONS ABOUT DSSTs

In order to pass the test, must I study from one of the recommended references?

The recommended references are a listing of books that were being used as textbooks in college courses of the same or similar title at the time the test was developed. Appropriate textbooks for study are not limited to those listed in the fact sheet. If you wish to obtain study resources to prepare for the examination, you may reference either the current edition of the listed titles or textbooks currently used at a local college or university for the same class title. It is recommended that you reference more than one textbook on the topics outlined in the fact sheet. You should begin by checking textbook content against the content outline included on the front page of the DSST fact sheet before selecting textbooks that cover the text content from which to study. Textbooks may be found at the campus bookstore of a local college or university offering a course on the subject.

Is there a penalty for guessing on the tests?

There is no penalty for guessing on DSSTs, so you should mark an answer for each question.

How much time will I have to complete the test?

Many DSSTs can be completed within 90 minutes; however, additional time can be allowed if necessary.

What should I do if I find a test question irregularity?

Continue testing and then report the irregularity to the test administrator after the test. This may be done by asking that the test administrator note the irregularity on the Supervisor's Irregularity Report or you can write to Thomson Prometric, DSST Program, 2000 Lenox Drive, Third Floor, Lawrenceville, NJ 08648, and indicate the form and question number(s) or circumstances as well as your name and address.

When will I receive my score report?

Allow approximately four weeks from the date of testing to receive your score report. Allow six to eight weeks to receive a score report for the *Principles of Public Speaking* examination.

Will my test scores be released without my permission?

Your test score will not be released to anyone other than the school you designate on your answer sheet unless you write to us and ask us to send a transcript elsewhere. Instructions about how to do this can be found on your score report. Your scores may be used for research purposes, but individual scores are never made public nor are individuals identified if research findings are made public.

If I do not achieve a passing score on the test, how long must I wait until I can take the test again?

If you do not receive a score on the test that will enable you to obtain credit for the course, you may take the test again after six months (180 days). Please do not attempt to take the test before six months (180 days) have passed because you will receive a score report marked <u>invalid</u> and your test fee will not be refunded.

Can my test scores be canceled?
The test administrator is required to report any irregularities to Thomson Prometric. <u>The consequence of bringing unauthorized materials into the testing room, or giving or receiving help, will be the forfeiture of your test fee and the invalidation of test scores.</u> The DSST Program reserves the right to cancel scores and not issue score reports in such situations.

What can I do if I feel that my test scores were not accurately reported?
Thomson Prometric recognizes the extreme importance of test results to candidates and has a multi-step quality-control procedure to help ensure that reported scores are accurate. If you have reason to believe that your score(s) were not accurately reported, you may request to have your answer sheet reviewed and hand scored.

The fees for this service are:
- $20 fee if requested within six months of the test date
- $30 fee if requested more than six months from the test date
- $30 fee if a re-evaluation of the *Principles of Public Speaking* speech is requested

The fee for this service can be paid by credit card or by certified check or U.S. money order payable to Thomson Prometric. Submit your request for score verification along with the appropriate fee or credit card information (credit card number and expiration date) to Thomson Prometric, DSST Program, 2000 Lenox Drive, Third Floor, Lawrenceville, NJ 08648. Include your full name, the test title, the date you took the test, and your Social Security number. Candidates will be notified if a scoring discrepancy is discovered within four weeks of receipt of the request.

What does ACE recommendation mean?
The ACE recommendation is the minimum passing score recommended by the American Council on Education for any given test. It is equivalent to the average score of students in the DSST norming sample who received a grade of C for the course. Some schools require a score higher than the ACE recommendation.

Who is NLC?
National Learning Corporation (NLC) has been successfully preparing candidates for 40 years for over 5,000 exams. NLC publishes Passbook® study guides to help candidates prepare for all DANTES and CLEP exams and almost every other type of exam from high school through adult career.

Go to our website — www.passbooks.com — or call (800) 632-8888 for information about ordering our Passbooks.

To get detailed information on the DSST program and DSST preparation materials, visit www.getcollegecredit.com.

If you are interested in taking the DSST exams, call 877-471-9860 or e-mail pnj-dsst@thomson.com.

DRUG AND ALCOHOL/SUBSTANCE ABUSE

EXAM INFORMATION

This exam was developed to enable schools to award credit to students for knowledge equivalent to that learned by students taking the course. This exam tests the understanding of such substances as anabolic steroids, over-the-counter medications, dependency/addiction, societal effects, screening, diagnosis and neurological factors.

The exam contains 100 questions to be answered in 2 hours.

CREDIT RECCMENDATIONS

The American Council on Education's College Credit Recommendation Service (ACE CREDIT) has evaluated the DSST test development process and content of this exam. It has made the following recommendations:

Area or Course Equivalent: Substance Abuse
Level: Upper-level baccalaureate
Amount of Credit: 3 Semester Hours
Minimum Score: 400

EXAM CONTENT OUTLINE

The following is an outline of the content areas covered in the examination. The approximate percentage of the examination devoted to each content area is also noted.

I. **Overview of Substance Abuse and Dependence — 12%**
   a. Terminology (e.g. abuse, use and misuse, dependency, psychological and physical addiction)
   b. Theories and models of abuse and dependence (e.g. genetic, psychological, social, cultural and environmental, moral, biopsychosocial disease)
   c. Demographics (e.g. age, gender, ethnicity, culture, socio-economic status)
   d. Costs to society and associations with social problems
   e. Screening and diagnosis (DSM-5)

II. **Classification of Drugs — 6%**
   a. DEA schedule
   b. Pharmacologic effect
   c. Regulations

III. **Pharmacological and Neurophysiological Principles — 9%**
   a. Nervous system (e.g. neurotransmission, synaptic processes, receptors)
   b. Actions of drugs (e.g. dose response curve, routes of administration, metabolism)
   c. Drug interactions

IV. **Alcohol — 14%**
   a. History and types
   b. Determinants of blood alcohol level (e.g. gender differences)
   c. Effects (e.g. acute, chronic, behavioral, physiological, prenatal)
   d. Uses and administration
   e. Tolerances, withdrawal and overdose
   f. Dependency issues
   g. Prevention and treatment (e.g. behavioral, pharmacological)

From the official announcement for educational purposes

V. **Anti-Anxiety, Sedative and Hypnotics – 6%**
   a. History and types
   b. Effects (e.g. acute, chronic, behavioral, physiological)
   c. Uses and administration
   d. Tolerance, withdrawal and overdose
   e. Dependency issues
   f. Prevention and treatment (e.g. behavioral pharmacological)

VI. **Inhalants – 5%**
   a. History and types
   b. Effects (e.g. acute, chronic, behavioral, physiological)
   c. Tolerance, Withdrawl, and Overdose
   d. Dependency Issues
   e. Prevention and Treatment (e.g. behavioral; pharmacological)

VII. **Tobacco and Nicotine – 10%**
   a. History and types
   b. Effects (e.g. acute, chronic, behavioral, physiological)
   c. Uses and administration
   d. Tolerance, withdrawal and overdose
   e. Dependency issues
   f. Prevention and treatment (e.g. behavioral pharmacological)

VIII. **Psychomotor – 6%**
   a. History and types (including caffeine and xanthines)
   b. Effects (e.g. acute, chronic, behavioral, physiological)
   c. Uses and administration
   d. Tolerance, withdrawal and overdose
   e. Dependency Issues
   f. Prevention and Treatment (e.g. behavioral pharmacological)

IX. **Opioids – 7%**
   a. History and types (including endogenous opioids)
   b. Effects (e.g. acute, chronic, behavioral physiological)
   c. Uses and administration
   d. Tolerance, withdrawal and overdose
   e. Dependency issues
   f. Prevention and treatment (e.g. behavioral; pharmacological)

X. **Cannabinoids – 10%**
   a. History and types (including endogenous cannabinoids)
   b. Effects (e.g. acute, chronic, behavioral; physiological)
   c. Uses and administration
   d. Tolerance, withdrawal and overdose
   e. Dependency issues
   f. Prevention and treatment (e.g. behavioral pharmacological)

XI. **Hallucinogens – 4%**
   a. History and types
   b. Effects (e.g. acute, chronic, behavioral, physiological)
   c. Uses and administration
   d. Tolerance, withdrawal and overdose

XII. **Other Drugs of Abuse – 4%**
   a. Anabolic steroids
   b. Over-the-counter (OTC) substances

4. Endorphins and enkephalins are similar in effect to?
   a. steroids
   b. psychedelics
   c. opiates
   d. stimulants

5. The metabolism of alcohol takes place primarily in the?
   a. liver
   b. kidneys
   c. brain
   d. pancreas

6. Crisis intervention and detection of the early stages of drug abuse is referred to as?
   a. primary prevention
   b. secondary prevention
   c. tertiary prevention
   d. quaternary prevention

7. Which of the following is an opium derivative?
   a. codeine
   b. cocaine
   c. phenobarbital
   d. LSD

8. The junction between two neurons is called the?
   a. axon
   b. dendrite
   c. synapse
   d. receptor

9. Paradoxical effects of the benzodiazepines include all of the following EXCEPT?
   a. nightmares
   b. irritability
   c. agitation
   d. hypersomnia

10. Buerger's disease caused by heavy cigarette smoking results from the?
    a. accumulation of tar in the lungs
    b. reduction of blood to the body's extremities
    c. destruction of the cilia in the trachea
    d. disruption of the normal functioning of the liver

11. An alcoholic who drinks while taking Antabuse (disulfiram) is likely to experience?
    a. sedation
    b. nausea
    c. convulsions
    d. euphoria

Answers to sample questions:
1-A, 2-A, 3-D, 4-C, 5-A, 6-B, 7-A, 8-C, 9-D, 10-B, 11-B

c. Synthetic substances
d. Club drugs

XII. Antipsychotic Drugs – 3%
a. History and types
b. Effects (including side effects, adverse reactions and toxicity)
c. Uses and administration

XIII. Antidepressants and Mood Stabilizers – 4%
a. History and types
b. Effects (including side effects, adverse reactions and toxicity)
c. Uses and administration
d. Tolerance, withdrawal and suicidal behaviors

REFERENCES
Below is a list of reference publications that were either used as a reference to create the exam, or were used as textbooks in college courses of the same or similar title at the time the test was developed. You may reference either the current edition of these titles or textbooks currently used at a local college or university for the same class title. It is recommended that you reference more than one textbook on the topics outlined in this fact sheet.

You should begin by checking textbook content against the content outline provided before selecting textbooks that cover the test content from which to study.

Sources for study material are suggested but not limited to the following:

1. *Drugs and Society,* 12th Edition, Glen Hanson, Peter J. Venturelli and Annette E. Fleckenstein, Jones and Bartlett Publishers.

2. *Drug, Society and Human Behavior,* 15th Edition, Har, Ksir and Ray, McGraw-Hill.

3. *Drug Behavior and Modern Society,* 8th Edition, Charles Levinthal.

SAMPLE QUESTIONS
All test questions are in a multiple-choice format, with one correct answer and three incorrect options. The following are samples of the types of questions that may appear on the exam.

1. Cannabis intoxication can?
    a. increase the heart rate
    b. increase mental activity
    c. cause respiratory collapse
    d. cause chromosomal damage

2. The drugs posing the most immediate risk of organic brain damage are?
    a. inhalants
    b. narcotics
    c. hallucinogens
    d. sedative hypnotics

3. The most commonly abused drug in the United State is?
    a. heroin
    b. cocaine
    c. marijuana
    d. alcohol

HOW TO TAKE A TEST

You have studied long, hard and conscientiously.

With your official admission card in hand, and your heart pounding, you have been admitted to the examination room.

You note that there are several hundred other applicants in the examination room waiting to take the same test.

They all appear to be equally well prepared.

You know that nothing but your best effort will suffice. The "moment of truth" is at hand: you now have to demonstrate objectively, in writing, your knowledge of content and your understanding of subject matter.

You are fighting the most important battle of your life—to pass and/or score high on an examination which will determine your career and provide the economic basis for your livelihood.

What extra, special things should you know and should you do in taking the examination?

I. YOU MUST PASS AN EXAMINATION

A. WHAT EVERY CANDIDATE SHOULD KNOW
   Examination applicants often ask us for help in preparing for the written test. What can I study in advance? What kinds of questions will be asked? How will the test be given? How will the papers be graded?

B. HOW ARE EXAMS DEVELOPED?
   Examinations are carefully written by trained technicians who are specialists in the field known as "psychological measurement," in consultation with recognized authorities in the field of work that the test will cover. These experts recommend the subject matter areas or skills to be tested; only those knowledges or skills important to your success on the job are included. The most reliable books and source materials available are used as references. Together, the experts and technicians judge the difficulty level of the questions.
   Test technicians know how to phrase questions so that the problem is clearly stated. Their ethics do not permit "trick" or "catch" questions. Questions may have been tried out on sample groups, or subjected to statistical analysis, to determine their usefulness.
   Written tests are often used in combination with performance tests, ratings of training and experience, and oral interviews. All of these measures combine to form the best-known means of finding the right person for the right job.

II. HOW TO PASS THE WRITTEN TEST

A. BASIC STEPS

1) Study the announcement

How, then, can you know what subjects to study? Our best answer is: "Learn as much as possible about the class of positions for which you've applied." The exam will test the knowledge, skills and abilities needed to do the work.

Your most valuable source of information about the position you want is the official exam announcement. This announcement lists the training and experience qualifications. Check these standards and apply only if you come reasonably close to meeting them. Many jurisdictions preview the written test in the exam announcement by including a section called "Knowledge and Abilities Required," "Scope of the Examination," or some similar heading. Here you will find out specifically what fields will be tested.

2) Choose appropriate study materials

If the position for which you are applying is technical or advanced, you will read more advanced, specialized material. If you are already familiar with the basic principles of your field, elementary textbooks would waste your time. Concentrate on advanced textbooks and technical periodicals. Think through the concepts and review difficult problems in your field.

These are all general sources. You can get more ideas on your own initiative, following these leads. For example, training manuals and publications of the government agency which employs workers in your field can be useful, particularly for technical and professional positions. A letter or visit to the government department involved may result in more specific study suggestions, and certainly will provide you with a more definite idea of the exact nature of the position you are seeking.

3) Study this book!

III. KINDS OF TESTS

Tests are used for purposes other than measuring knowledge and ability to perform specified duties. For some positions, it is equally important to test ability to make adjustments to new situations or to profit from training. In others, basic mental abilities not dependent on information are essential. Questions which test these things may not appear as pertinent to the duties of the position as those which test for knowledge and information. Yet they are often highly important parts of a fair examination. For very general questions, it is almost impossible to help you direct your study efforts. What we can do is to point out some of the more common of these general abilities needed in public service positions and describe some typical questions.

1) General information

Broad, general information has been found useful for predicting job success in some kinds of work. This is tested in a variety of ways, from vocabulary lists to questions about current events. Basic background in some field of work, such as sociology or economics, may be sampled in a group of questions. Often these are principles which have become familiar to most persons through exposure rather than through formal training. It is difficult to advise you how to study for these questions; being alert to the world around you is our best suggestion.

2) Verbal ability

An example of an ability needed in many positions is verbal or language ability. Verbal ability is, in brief, the ability to use and understand words. Vocabulary and grammar tests are typical measures of this ability. Reading comprehension or paragraph interpretation questions are common in many kinds of civil service tests. You are given a paragraph of written material and asked to find its central meaning.

IV. KINDS OF QUESTIONS

1. Multiple-choice Questions

Most popular of the short-answer questions is the "multiple choice" or "best answer" question. It can be used, for example, to test for factual knowledge, ability to solve problems or judgment in meeting situations found at work.

A multiple-choice question is normally one of three types:
- It can begin with an incomplete statement followed by several possible endings. You are to find the one ending which best completes the statement, although some of the others may not be entirely wrong.
- It can also be a complete statement in the form of a question which is answered by choosing one of the statements listed.
- It can be in the form of a problem – again you select the best answer.

Here is an example of a multiple-choice question with a discussion which should give you some clues as to the method for choosing the right answer:

When an employee has a complaint about his assignment, the action which will best help him overcome his difficulty is to
- A. discuss his difficulty with his coworkers
- B. take the problem to the head of the organization
- C. take the problem to the person who gave him the assignment
- D. say nothing to anyone about his complaint

In answering this question, you should study each of the choices to find which is best. Consider choice "A" – Certainly an employee may discuss his complaint with fellow employees, but no change or improvement can result, and the complaint remains unresolved. Choice "B" is a poor choice since the head of the organization probably does not know what assignment you have been given, and taking your problem to him is known as "going over the head" of the supervisor. The supervisor, or person who made the assignment, is the person who can clarify it or correct any injustice. Choice "C" is, therefore, correct. To say nothing, as in choice "D," is unwise. Supervisors have and interest in knowing the problems employees are facing, and the employee is seeking a solution to his problem.

2. True/False

3. Matching Questions

Matching an answer from a column of choices within another column.

V. RECORDING YOUR ANSWERS

Computer terminals are used more and more today for many different kinds of exams.

For an examination with very few applicants, you may be told to record your answers in the test booklet itself. Separate answer sheets are much more common. If this separate answer sheet is to be scored by machine – and this is often the case – it is highly important that you mark your answers correctly in order to get credit.

VI. BEFORE THE TEST

YOUR PHYSICAL CONDITION IS IMPORTANT

If you are not well, you can't do your best work on tests. If you are half asleep, you can't do your best either. Here are some tips:

1) Get about the same amount of sleep you usually get. Don't stay up all night before the test, either partying or worrying—DON'T DO IT!
2) If you wear glasses, be sure to wear them when you go to take the test. This goes for hearing aids, too.
3) If you have any physical problems that may keep you from doing your best, be sure to tell the person giving the test. If you are sick or in poor health, you relay cannot do your best on any test. You can always come back and take the test some other time.

Common sense will help you find procedures to follow to get ready for an examination. Too many of us, however, overlook these sensible measures. Indeed, nervousness and fatigue have been found to be the most serious reasons why applicants fail to do their best on civil service tests. Here is a list of reminders:

- Begin your preparation early – Don't wait until the last minute to go scurrying around for books and materials or to find out what the position is all about.
- Prepare continuously – An hour a night for a week is better than an all-night cram session. This has been definitely established. What is more, a night a week for a month will return better dividends than crowding your study into a shorter period of time.
- Locate the place of the exam – You have been sent a notice telling you when and where to report for the examination. If the location is in a different town or otherwise unfamiliar to you, it would be well to inquire the best route and learn something about the building.
- Relax the night before the test – Allow your mind to rest. Do not study at all that night. Plan some mild recreation or diversion; then go to bed early and get a good night's sleep.
- Get up early enough to make a leisurely trip to the place for the test – This way unforeseen events, traffic snarls, unfamiliar buildings, etc. will not upset you.
- Dress comfortably – A written test is not a fashion show. You will be known by number and not by name, so wear something comfortable.
- Leave excess paraphernalia at home – Shopping bags and odd bundles will get in your way. You need bring only the items mentioned in the official notice you received; usually everything you need is provided. Do not bring reference books to the exam. They will only confuse those last minutes and be taken away from you when in the test room.

- Arrive somewhat ahead of time – If because of transportation schedules you must get there very early, bring a newspaper or magazine to take your mind off yourself while waiting.
- Locate the examination room – When you have found the proper room, you will be directed to the seat or part of the room where you will sit. Sometimes you are given a sheet of instructions to read while you are waiting. Do not fill out any forms until you are told to do so; just read them and be prepared.
- Relax and prepare to listen to the instructions
- If you have any physical problem that may keep you from doing your best, be sure to tell the test administrator. If you are sick or in poor health, you really cannot do your best on the exam. You can come back and take the test some other time.

VII. AT THE TEST

The day of the test is here and you have the test booklet in your hand. The temptation to get going is very strong. Caution! There is more to success than knowing the right answers. You must know how to identify your papers and understand variations in the type of short-answer question used in this particular examination. Follow these suggestions for maximum results from your efforts:

1) Cooperate with the monitor

The test administrator has a duty to create a situation in which you can be as much at ease as possible. He will give instructions, tell you when to begin, check to see that you are marking your answer sheet correctly, and so on. He is not there to guard you, although he will see that your competitors do not take unfair advantage. He wants to help you do your best.

2) Listen to all instructions

Don't jump the gun! Wait until you understand all directions. In most civil service tests you get more time than you need to answer the questions. So don't be in a hurry. Read each word of instructions until you clearly understand the meaning. Study the examples, listen to all announcements and follow directions. Ask questions if you do not understand what to do.

3) Identify your papers

Civil service exams are usually identified by number only. You will be assigned a number; you must not put your name on your test papers. Be sure to copy your number correctly. Since more than one exam may be given, copy your exact examination title.

4) Plan your time

Unless you are told that a test is a "speed" or "rate of work" test, speed itself is usually not important. Time enough to answer all the questions will be provided, but this does not mean that you have all day. An overall time limit has been set. Divide the total time (in minutes) by the number of questions to determine the approximate time you have for each question.

5) Do not linger over difficult questions

If you come across a difficult question, mark it with a paper clip (useful to have along) and come back to it when you have been through the booklet. One caution if you do this – be sure to skip a number on your answer sheet as well. Check often to be sure that you have not lost your place and that you are marking in the row numbered the same as the question you are answering.

6) Read the questions

Be sure you know what the question asks! Many capable people are unsuccessful because they failed to read the questions correctly.

7) Answer all questions

Unless you have been instructed that a penalty will be deducted for incorrect answers, it is better to guess than to omit a question.

8) Speed tests

It is often better NOT to guess on speed tests. It has been found that on timed tests people are tempted to spend the last few seconds before time is called in marking answers at random – without even reading them – in the hope of picking up a few extra points. To discourage this practice, the instructions may warn you that your score will be "corrected" for guessing. That is, a penalty will be applied. The incorrect answers will be deducted from the correct ones, or some other penalty formula will be used.

9) Review your answers

If you finish before time is called, go back to the questions you guessed or omitted to give them further thought. Review other answers if you have time.

10) Return your test materials

If you are ready to leave before others have finished or time is called, take ALL your materials to the monitor and leave quietly. Never take any test material with you. The monitor can discover whose papers are not complete, and taking a test booklet may be grounds for disqualification.

VIII. EXAMINATION TECHNIQUES

1) Read the general instructions carefully. These are usually printed on the first page of the exam booklet. As a rule, these instructions refer to the timing of the examination; the fact that you should not start work until the signal and must stop work at a signal, etc. If there are any special instructions, such as a choice of questions to be answered, make sure that you note this instruction carefully.

2) When you are ready to start work on the examination, that is as soon as the signal has been given, read the instructions to each question booklet, underline any key words or phrases, such as least, best, outline, describe and the like. In this way you will tend to answer as requested rather than discover on reviewing your paper that you listed without describing, that you selected the worst choice rather than the best choice, etc.

3) If the examination is of the objective or multiple-choice type – that is, each question will also give a series of possible answers: A, B, C or D, and you are called upon to select the best answer and write the letter next to that answer on your answer paper – it is advisable to start answering each question in turn. There may be anywhere from 50 to 100 such questions in the three or four hours allotted and you can see how much time would be taken if you read through all the questions before beginning to answer any. Furthermore, if you

come across a question or group of questions which you know would be difficult to answer, it would undoubtedly affect your handling of all the other questions.

4) If the examination is of the essay type and contains but a few questions, it is a moot point as to whether you should read all the questions before starting to answer any one. Of course, if you are given a choice – say five out of seven and the like – then it is essential to read all the questions so you can eliminate the two that are most difficult. If, however, you are asked to answer all the questions, there may be danger in trying to answer the easiest one first because you may find that you will spend too much time on it. The best technique is to answer the first question, then proceed to the second, etc.

5) Time your answers. Before the exam begins, write down the time it started, then add the time allowed for the examination and write down the time it must be completed, then divide the time available somewhat as follows:
   - If 3-1/2 hours are allowed, that would be 210 minutes. If you have 80 objective-type questions, that would be an average of 2-1/2 minutes per question. Allow yourself no more than 2 minutes per question, or a total of 160 minutes, which will permit about 50 minutes to review.
   - If for the time allotment of 210 minutes there are 7 essay questions to answer, that would average about 30 minutes a question. Give yourself only 25 minutes per question so that you have about 35 minutes to review.

6) The most important instruction is to read each question and make sure you know what is wanted. The second most important instruction is to time yourself properly so that you answer every question. The third most important instruction is to answer every question. Guess if you have to but include something for each question. Remember that you will receive no credit for a blank and will probably receive some credit if you write something in answer to an essay question. If you guess a letter – say "B" for a multiple-choice question – you may have guessed right. If you leave a blank as an answer to a multiple-choice question, the examiners may respect your feelings but it will not add a point to your score. Some exams may penalize you for wrong answers, so in such cases only, you may not want to guess unless you have some basis for your answer.

7) Suggestions
   a. Objective-type questions
      1. Examine the question booklet for proper sequence of pages and questions
      2. Read all instructions carefully
      3. Skip any question which seems too difficult; return to it after all other questions have been answered
      4. Apportion your time properly; do not spend too much time on any single question or group of questions
      5. Note and underline key words – all, most, fewest, least, best, worst, same, opposite, etc.
      6. Pay particular attention to negatives
      7. Note unusual option, e.g., unduly long, short, complex, different or similar in content to the body of the question
      8. Observe the use of "hedging" words – probably, may, most likely, etc.

9. Make sure that your answer is put next to the same number as the question
10. Do not second-guess unless you have good reason to believe the second answer is definitely more correct
11. Cross out original answer if you decide another answer is more accurate; do not erase until you are ready to hand your paper in
12. Answer all questions; guess unless instructed otherwise
13. Leave time for review

b. Essay questions
1. Read each question carefully
2. Determine exactly what is wanted. Underline key words or phrases.
3. Decide on outline or paragraph answer
4. Include many different points and elements unless asked to develop any one or two points or elements
5. Show impartiality by giving pros and cons unless directed to select one side only
6. Make and write down any assumptions you find necessary to answer the questions
7. Watch your English, grammar, punctuation and choice of words
8. Time your answers; don't crowd material

8) Answering the essay question

Most essay questions can be answered by framing the specific response around several key words or ideas. Here are a few such key words or ideas:

M's: manpower, materials, methods, money, management
P's: purpose, program, policy, plan, procedure, practice, problems, pitfalls, personnel, public relations

a. Six basic steps in handling problems:
1. Preliminary plan and background development
2. Collect information, data and facts
3. Analyze and interpret information, data and facts
4. Analyze and develop solutions as well as make recommendations
5. Prepare report and sell recommendations
6. Install recommendations and follow up effectiveness

b. Pitfalls to avoid
1. Taking things for granted – A statement of the situation does not necessarily imply that each of the elements is necessarily true; for example, a complaint may be invalid and biased so that all that can be taken for granted is that a complaint has been registered
2. Considering only one side of a situation – Wherever possible, indicate several alternatives and then point out the reasons you selected the best one
3. Failing to indicate follow up – Whenever your answer indicates action on your part, make certain that you will take proper follow-up action to see how successful your recommendations, procedures or actions turn out to be
4. Taking too long in answering any single question – Remember to time your answers properly

EXAMINATION SECTION

EXAMINATION SECTION
TEST 1

DIRECTIONS: Each question or incomplete statement is followed by several suggested answers or completions. Select the one that BEST answers the question or completes the statement. *PRINT THE LETTER OF THE CORRECT ANSWER IN THE SPACE AT THE RIGHT*

1. According to the federal government, the estimated annual economic cost of drug abuse in the United States is closest to

    A. $500 million
    B. $4 billion
    C. $180 billion
    D. $1.2 trillion

1._____

2. Which of the following is an anesthetic inhalant?

    A. Xylene
    B. Nitrous oxide
    C. Amyl nitrite
    D. Toluene

2._____

3. Short-term effects of marijuana use include

    A. reduced heart rate
    B. increased blood pressure
    C. bronchitis
    D. increased appetite

3._____

4. The first alkaloid ever isolated from the opium poppy was

    A. morphine
    B. codeine
    C. heroin
    D. methadone

4._____

5. In the United States, the most effective drug abuse prevention efforts have typically focused on

    A. peer and social influences
    B. real-life case studies
    C. worst-case scenarios
    D. legal rationales

5._____

6. Fatal consequences, although rare, are possible for those who suddenly stop their chronic use of _____ without medical supervision.
    I. barbiturates
    II. alcohol
    III. cocaine
    IV. heroin

6._____

1

A. I or II
B. II only
C. I, II or IV
D. I, II, III or IV

7. The use of drugs or alcohol to avoid withdrawal symptoms is an example of

   A. potentiation
   B. positive reinforcement
   C. negative tolerance
   D. negative reinforcement

7.____

8. The barbiturates are typically classified according to their

   A. duration of action
   B. potential for interaction with alcohol
   C. method of metabolism
   D. chemical structure

8.____

9. Which of the following is a club drag that stimulates the release of human growth hormone, and whose main ingredient is an industrial solvent?

   A. GHB (gamma hydroxybutyrate)
   B. GABA (ganima-aminobutyric acid)
   C. MDMA (ecstasy)
   D. Ketamine

9.____

10. Typically, heroin is about_____times stronger than morphine.

    A. 1-2
    B. 3-10
    C. 5-20
    D. 40

10.____

11. Among the following groups, the highest rates of illicit drug use are reported among

    A. construction workers
    B. physicians and nurses
    C. law enforcement officers
    D. social sendee professionals

11.____

12. It is estimated that about _____ percent of patients who suffer from a form of mental illness also have a substance abuse disorder.

    A. 10-20
    B. 25-35
    C. 40-75
    D. 70-85

12.____

13. The indirect effects of alcohol consumption are illustrated by the

    A. decrease in thiamin absorption
    B. increased risk of fetal alcohol syndrome among pregnant women

13.____

C. relationship between drinking and motor vehicle crashes
D. relationship between drinking and liver cancer

14. Which of the following is classified as a deliriant?

    A. Psilocybin
    B. Mescaline
    C. Datura
    D. LSD

15. Most first-time drinkers would likely be passed out by the time their blood alcohol content reaches _____ %.

    A. .05
    B. .08
    C. .15
    D. .20

16. Each of the following neurotransmitters is thought to play a role in a person's biological predisposition toward alcoholism, EXCEPT

    A. GABA
    B. norepinephrine
    C. serotonin
    D. dopamine

17. Typically, the alcohol in a drink will reach the bloodstream in about _____ minutes.

    A. 15
    B. 30
    C. 45
    D. 60

18. Which of the following drugs is used to treat manic symptoms?

    A. Lithium
    B. Methadone
    C. Paxil
    D. Librium

19. _____ drugs typically act by blocking the brain's dopamine receptors.

    A. Antipsychotic
    B. Steroidal
    C. Analgesic
    D. Opioid

20. For U.S. adolescents in a substance treatment program, the primary drug of abuse is most likely to be

    A. marijuana
    B. an inhalant
    C. alcohol
    D. cocaine

21. In 1988 the Anti-Drug Abuse Act created the government agency known as the

    A. White House Office of National Drug Control Policy (ONDCP)
    B. Substance Abuse and Mental Health Services Administration (SAMH-SA)
    C. Drug Enforcement Agency (DEA)
    D. National Institute on Drag Abuse (NIDA)

22. Babies whose mothers have used cocaine during pregnancy are likely to have a higher rate of

    I. low birth weight
    II. sudden infant death syndrome (SIDS)
    III. genito-urinary malformations
    IV. congenital heart delects

    A. I and II
    B. II and III
    C. II and IV
    D. I, II, III and IV

23. A "Type I" alcoholic generally has each of the following personality traits, EXCEPT

    A. optimism
    B. rigidity in behaviors and beliefs
    C. shyness
    D. sentimentality

24. Each of the following is a commonly occurring effect of chronic opiate dosing, EXCEPT

    A. weightless
    B. increased urination
    C. constricted pupils
    D. elevated body temperature

25. The late stages of alcoholism are often characterized by

    A. reverse tolerance
    B. synergism
    C. pharmacological tolerance
    D. cross-tolerance

KEY (CORRECT ANSWERS)

1. C
2. B
3. D
4. A
5. A

6. C
7. D
8. A
9. A
10. B

11. A
12. C
13. C
14. C
15. C

16. B
17. A
18. A
19. A
20. A

21. A
22. D
23. A
24. C
25. A

TEST 2

DIRECTIONS: Each question or incomplete statement is followed by several suggested answers or completions. Select the one that BEST answers the question or completes the statement. *PRINT THE LETTER OF THE CORRECT ANSWER IN THE SPACE AT THE RIGHT.*

1. Alcohol withdrawal differs significantly from withdrawal from other drugs in that it

    A. can result in hallucinations
    B. is purely psychological
    C. can be directly fatal
    D. is treatable with synthetic opioids

    1.____

2. Although the terms "opioid" and "opiate" are often used interchangeably, "opiate" more properly refers only to

    A. opioids that are produced naturally by an organism
    B. natural opium alkaloids and the semi-synthetics derived from them.
    C. an opioid that is used only as prescribed
    D. fully synthetic opioids

    2.____

3. Ingesting/injecting several anabolic steroids at once is referred to as

    A. stacking
    B. cycling
    C. chipping
    D. raging

    3.____

4. Over the years, research has suggested that women who drink heavily die an average of _____ years earlier than women who do not drink at all.

    A. 5
    B. 10
    C. 15
    D. 25

    4.____

5. The first stage of barbiturate withdrawal, the "delirium" stage, lasts for about

    A. 12 hours
    B. 48 hours
    C. 5 days
    D. 10 days

    5.____

6. NMDA receptor antagonists include
    I. PCP
    II. ketamine
    III. psilocybin
    IV. LSD

    A. I only
    B. I and II
    C. II and III
    D. LSD

    6.____

7. Rebound insomnia, in which a person has greater difficulty falling asleep, is often associated with the use of

   A. stimulants
   B. sedative hypnotics
   C. hallucinogens
   D. narcotics

8. A single marijuana cigarette is associated with about _____ the bronchial damage associated with a regular tobacco cigarette.

   A. half
   B. the same
   C. 4 times
   D. 20 times

9. A drug that is described as "diuretic"

   A. softens the stool and makes defecation easier
   B. is used to treat heart arrhythmias
   C. accelerates the elimination of fluid
   D. slows the elimination of fluid

10. As of 2007, Rohypnol is a Schedule _____ substance.

    A. I
    B. II
    C. III
    D. IV

11. If a drug is said to have a therapeutic index of 1:4, that means that

    A. the effective dose is 1/4 of the lethal dose.
    B. only 1 person in 4 can safely use the drug.
    C. the drug remains effective for 1-4 hours.
    D. only 1/4 of the effective dose is biotransformed every hour.

12. Between a third and two-thirds of all child-welfare cases in the United States involve

    A. child substance abuse
    B. parental substance abuse
    C. prenatal substance exposure
    D. parental tobacco use

13. Methamphetanine is sometimes prescribed today for the treatment of

    A. atrial fibrillation
    B. insomnia
    C. depression
    D. attention deficit/hyperactivity disorder (ADHD)

14. Which of the following drug abuse prevention methods teaches students to recognize, manage, and avoid situations that might involve drug abuse?

A. Resistance skills training
B. Values clarification
C. Negative reinforcement
D. Self-efficacy training

15. In the United States, about _____ percent of all primary care and hospitalized patients suffer from alcohol dependence.

    A. 5 to 7
    B. 15 to 20
    C. 25 to 40
    D. 35 to 50

16. Which of the following is NOT a common sign of barbiturate use?

    A. Constricted pupils
    B. Cyanosis
    C. Cold, clammy skin
    D. Muscle twitches

17. In a given day, about _____ Americans receive treatment for alcoholism.

    A. 700,000
    B. 1.2 million
    C. 3.4 million
    D. 6 million

18. Drugs that are known for their relatively narrow therapeutic window, or margin of safety, include
    I. digoxin
    II. lithium carbonate
    III. opioids
    IV. acetaminophen

    A. I and II
    B. I, II and IV
    C. III only
    D. I, II and III

19. The class of drugs with the fewest accepted medical uses are the

    A. hallucinogens
    B. stimulants
    C. anabolic steroids
    D. opioids

20. Which of the following is most commonly associated with stroke, lung and liver damage, and sudden death due to cardiac arrest?

    A. Ketamine
    B. Ecstasy
    C. Marijuana
    D. Cocaine

21. Quaalude, a barbiturate alternative, is a brand name for the drug

    A. mefloquine
    B. quinine
    C. methaqualone
    D. quazepam

22. The median lethal dose for alcohol is a blood alcohol content (BAC) of about _____ percent.

    A. .20
    B. .40
    C. .60
    D. .80

23. Which of the following is a powerful opiate known by the slang term "China White"?

    A. Morphine
    B. Darvon
    C. Percocet
    D. Fentanyl

24. When a person's average number of drinks per day are plotted on the horizontal axis of a graph, beginning with "zero" in the lower left corner, and the risk of death is plotted upward on the vertical axis, the result is a(n)

    A. J-shaped curve
    B. straight diagonal line traveling to the upper right
    C. M-shaped curve
    D. bell curve

25. An example of a "harm reduction" policy approach to drug abuse is

    A. mandatory diversions
    B. needle-exchange programs
    C. education programs
    D. decriminalization

KEY (CORRECT ANSWERS)

1.	C		11.	A
2.	B		12.	B
3.	A		13.	D
4.	C		14.	A
5.	C		15.	B
6.	B		16.	A
7.	B		17.	A
8.	D		18.	B
9.	C		19.	A
10.	D		20.	D

21. C
22. B
23. D
24. A
25. B

TEST 3

DIRECTIONS: Each question or incomplete statement is followed by several suggested answers or completions. Select the one that BEST answers the question or completes the statement. *PRINT THE LETTER OF THE CORRECT ANSWER IN THE SPACE AT THE RIGHT.*

1. In the United States, illicit drag use is most prevalent in

    A. inner city areas
    B. the suburbs
    C. rural areas
    D. the Midwest

   1.____

2. The goal of the intervention process is to

    A. convince the person that he or she needs treatment
    B. identify the person's primary defense mechanism
    C. isolate the client to make him or her feel the consequences of behavior
    D. establish a working relationship with the physician or substance abuse counselor

   2.____

3. Typically, about _____ percent of alcohol-dependent people seek treatment for their disorder.

    A. 10
    B. 25
    C. 35
    D. 50

   3.____

4. The word "flip," in varying forms, is often used to describe a combination of the drug _____ with another recreational drug.

    A. ecstasy (MDMA)
    B. cocaine
    C. LSD
    D. marijuana

   4.____

5. Which of the following does NOT bind with the brain's serotonin receptors?

    A. LSD
    B. Haloperidol
    C. Psilocybin
    D. DMT

   5.____

6. The Fourth Edition of the Diagnostic and Statistical Manual of Mental Disorderscommonly known as the DSM-IV and published by the American Psychiatric Associationincludes each of the following in its criteria for a diagnosis of drug or alcohol dependency, EXCEPT

    A. developing a tolerance for the substance
    B. preoccupation with further use of the substance
    C. using the substance solely in moments of peak stress
    D. using the substance at inappropriate times

   6.____

7. Neurotransmitters is involved in the voluntary movement of muscles include
    I. epinephrine
    II. dopamine
    III. acetylcholine
    IV. GABA

    A. I and II
    B. II and III
    C. II, III and IV
    D. I, II, III and IV

8. The psychoactive agent in permanent markers that are sniffed or inhaled is

    A. acetone
    B. xylene
    C. ether
    D. butane

9. Minor tranquilizers, nonbarbiturate sedatives, and barbiturates are classified as

    A. sedative hypnotics
    B. psychedelics
    C. benzodiazepines
    D. inhalants

10. Other than methadone, which of the following is a synthetic drug approved for treating narcotic withdrawal?

    A. GHB
    B. Fentanyl
    C. LAAM
    D. Thiamine

11. The psychological trait most often linked with drug use is

    A. antisocial personality disorder
    B. low self-esteem
    C. impulsiveness
    D. denial

12. The smallest amount of a drug required to produce an effect is called the _____ dose.

    A. therapeutic
    B. standard
    C. threshold
    D. marginal

13. As a group, the ethnicity that typically records the lowest alcohol consumption in the United States is

    A. Asian Americans
    B. Hispanic Americans
    C. Euro-Americans
    D. African Americans

14. Injecting cocaine provides the highest blood levels of the drug in the shortest amount of time, but is generally avoided by users because it

    A. tends to cause immediate unconsciousness
    B. is very dangerous
    C. results in a loss of motor control
    D. tends to cause uncontrollable vomiting

    14._____

15. Physiological symptoms associated with heroin use include
    I. vomiting
    II. sleepiness
    III. constipation
    IV. reduced sex drive

    A. I and II
    B. II only
    C. II and III
    D. I, II, III and IV

    15._____

16. Each of the following has been classified as a psychedelic drug, EXCEPT

    A. Ketamine
    B. LSD
    C. marijuana
    D. ecstasy (MDMA)

    16._____

17. During the hour after cocaine is used, the risk of heart attack increases by a factor of about

    A. 5
    B. 10
    C. 25
    D. 50

    17._____

18. Tricyclic drags, when combined with _____ , may produce a fatal reaction.

    A. LSD
    B. benzodiazepines
    C. alcohol
    D. narcotics

    18._____

19. Which of the following is NOT a health risk associated with alcoholism?

    A. Bladder cancer
    B. Pancreatitis
    C. Hypertension
    D. Breast cancer

    19._____

20. Statistics show that most people in drug or alcohol treatment programs throughout the United States

    A. use primarily one drug of choice
    B. are unlikely to use again after completing the program

    20._____

C. use more than one substance
D. are between the ages of 35 and 44

21. The age group most likely to abuse inhalants is

    A. 12-17
    B. 18-25
    C. 25-44
    D. 45-60

22. Under the Controlled Substances Act, benzodiazepines are Schedule _____.

    A. I
    B. II
    C. III
    D. IV

23. A single drink containing one ounce (28 grams) of alcohol will increase the average person's BAC by roughly _____ percent.

    A. .01
    B. .03
    C. .05
    D. .07

24. Withdrawal from THC is commonly associated with each of the following, EXCEPT

    A. nausea
    B. paranoia
    C. insomnia
    D. loss of appetite

25. When a pregnant woman drinks alcohol, the fetal blood alcohol will equal the mother's in about

    A. 15 minutes
    B. 1 hour
    C. 3 hours
    D. 6 hours

KEY (CORRECT ANSWERS)

1.	A	11.	D
2.	A	12.	C
3.	A	13.	A
4.	A	14.	D
5.	B	15.	D
6.	C	16.	A
7.	C	17.	C
8.	B	18.	C
9.	A	19.	A
10.	C	20.	C
21.	A		
22.	D		
23.	B		
24.	B		
25.	A		

TEST 4

DIRECTIONS: Each question or incomplete statement is followed by several suggested answers or completions. Select the one that BEST answers the question or completes the statement. *PRINT THE LETTER OF THE CORRECT ANSWER IN THE SPACE AT THE RIGHT.*

1. In the United States, about _____ percent of the convicts housed in federal prisons are there because of drug-related crimes.   1.____

    A. 10
    B. 30
    C. 50
    D. 70

2. Which of the following is NOT an opioid?   2.____

    A. Codeine
    B. Oxycodone
    C. Heroin
    D. Cocaine

3. Marijuana is most likely to be used medically as a(n)   3.____

    A. anti-emetic
    B. laxative
    C. anti-inflammatory
    D. diuretic

4. The brain's center of arousal and motivation, and attention is known as the   4.____

    A. reticular activating system
    B. limbic system
    C. frontal cortex
    D. basal ganglia

5. Which of the following is a brand name for a benzodiazepine most commonly used to induce sleep?   5.____

    A. Xanax
    B. Valium
    C. Librium
    D. Halcion

6. The class of drugs known as hypnotics typically includes   6.____
    I. GHB
    II. benzodiazepines
    III. opiates
    IV. barbiturates

    A. I and II
    B. I, III and IV
    C. II and IV
    D. I, II, III and IV

16

7. It usually takes about _____ for inhaled drugs to reach the brain.

    A. less than a second
    B. 5-8 seconds
    C. 20-30 seconds
    D. 1-3 minutes

8. What is the term for a chemical substance that crosses a synapse to a receptor site?

    A. Hormone
    B. Dendrite
    C. Neurotransmitter
    D. Agonist

9. Which of the following is NOT classified as a dissociative anesthetic drug?

    A. Psilocybin
    B. Ketamine
    C. Phencyclidine (PCP)
    D. Dextromethorphan

10. For at-risk students in the United States, the most effective drug abuse prevention programs are usually _____ in their approach.

    A. confrontational
    B. alternative
    C. highly structured
    D. peer-led

11. Heavy consumption of alcohol reduces the production of the neuroinhibito

    A. GABA
    B. glutamate
    C. glycine
    D. NDMA

12. In the United States of the early 21st century, the drug of abuse most likely to be administered intravenously was

    A. cocaine
    B. Flunitrazepam (Rohypnol)
    C. methamphetamine
    D. heroin

13. Of the following physical effects of narcotics, the LEAST common is

    A. dry mouth
    B. nausea
    C. respiratory depression
    D. constipation

14. The "controlled drinking" approach to treating alcoholism is not recommended for people with

A. little or no social support
B. functional problems related to alcoholism
C. liver disease
D. cancer

15. The route of administration for anabolic steroids that showed the largest growth in popularity during the early 21st century was

A. intravenous injection
B. intramuscular injection
C. creams, gels, and transdermal patches
D. oral ingestion

16. Of the following routes of administration, which is LEAST likely to lead to overdose?

A. Injecting
B. Smoking
C. Swallowing
D. Snorting

17. In the United States, a blood alcohol concentration reported as .20% means specifically that

A. every 100 milliliters of a person's blood contains .02 grams of alcohol
B. every 1000 grams of a person's blood contains 2 grams of alcohol
C. every 200 grams of a person's blood contains a milliliter of alcohol
D. every 1000 milliliters of a person's blood contains .02 milliliters of blood

18. The increasing use of inhalants by American teenagers has been largely attributed to

A. the low cost and availability of inhalants
B. a lack of clear regulation regarding their use
C. a celebrity culture that glorifies the use of inhalants
D. the increasing refinement of inhalants that produce euphoria

19. When abused, methamphetamines are especially harmful to the _____ system.

A. gastrointestinal
B. dental
C. autonomic nervous
D. cardiovascular

20. At the beginning of the 21st century, the world's largest producer of illegal opium was

A. Myanmar
B. Colombia
C. Afghanistan
D. China

21. Another term for antipsychotic drugs is

A. minor tranquilizers
B. benzodiazepines

C. major tranquilizers
D. hypnotics

22. Chronic alcohol use affects the body's immune system in each of the following ways, EXCEPT by

    A. increasing the susceptibility to infection
    B. inhibiting white blood cells
    C. interfering with recovery from colds and flu
    D. increasing red blood cell counts

23. Each of the following has been linked to steroid use, EXCEPT

    A. Liver and kidney cancer
    B. Pancreatitis
    C. Low sperm count
    D. Abrupt mood swings

24. In the last half-century, the medical community has been most significantly influenced by the _____ model as the explanation for why people abuse alcohol.

    A. social learning
    B. disease
    C. stress-response-dampening
    D. tension reduction

25. The Drug Abuse Warning Network (DAWN) is a system that

    A. seeks to discourage interest in illegal drugs, gangs, and violence through education
    B. improves the quality and availability of prevention, treatment, and rehabilitative services in order to reduce illness, death, disability, and cost to society resulting from substance abuse and mental illness
    C. monitors drug-related visits to hospital emergency departments and drug-related deaths investigated by medical examiners and coroners
    D. establishes policies, priorities, and objectives to eradicate illicit drug use, manufacturing, and trafficking, drug-related crime and violence, and drug-related health consequences in the United States

KEY (CORRECT ANSWERS)

1. C
2. D
3. A
4. A
5. D

6. C
7. B
8. C
9. A
10. B

11. A
12. C
13. C
14. C
15. C

16. C
17. A
18. A
19. D
20. C

21. C
22. D
23. B
24. B
25. C

EXAMINATION SECTION
TEST 1

DIRECTIONS: Each question or incomplete statement is followed by several suggested answers or completions. Select the one that BEST answers the question or completes the statement. *PRINT THE LETTER OF THE CORRECT ANSWER IN THE SPACE AT THE RIGHT.*

1. Which of the following benzodiazepines is treated most strictly by the federal government? 1.____

    A. Flunitrazepam (Rohypnol)
    B. Diazepam (Valium)
    C. Chlordiazepoxide (Librium)
    D. Alprazolam (Xanax)

2. Which of the following neurotransmitters generally governs a person's wakefulness and arousal, and is involved in the "fight or flight" response? 2.____

    A. Acetylcholine
    B. Norepinephrine
    C. Dopamine
    D. Serotonin

3. Another name for anticholinergic substances is 3.____

    A. dissociatives
    B. deliriants
    C. cannabinoids
    D. hormones

4. Which of the following terms is used to denote efforts to halt the import, sale, and manufacture of illicit drugs? 4.____

    A. Narcoterrorism
    B. Diversion
    C. Customs
    D. Interdiction

5. The psychoactive substance found in the peyote cactus is 5.____

    A. ketamine
    B. mescaline
    C. phencyclidine
    D. psilocybin

6. Drugs that are used to treat the symptoms of alcoholic withdrawal include 6.____
    I. Librium
    II. phenobarbital
    III. methadone
    IV. disulfiram

    A. I and II   B. II only   C. II, III and IV   D. I, II, III and IV

7. Which of the following drugs is used to stabilize the chemical balance of the brain, which would otherwise be disrupted by alcoholism?

    A. Acaraprosate (Campral)
    B. Naltrexone
    C. Baclofen
    D. Disulfiram (Antabuse)

8. Marijuana is known to affect the _____ , or the part of the brain that controls memory.

    A. cerebellum
    B. hippocampus
    C. pons
    D. hypothalamus

9. The most common cause of impotence among middle-aged men is

    A. overuse of stimulants
    B. nicotine addiction
    C. high blood pressure
    D. alcohol overuse

10. In medicine, narcotic analgesics are favored over other types of painkillers because they involve fewer adverse affects on

    A. the synaptic response
    B. the gastrointestinal system
    C. memory
    D. intellectual and motor function

11. A person's perception and judgement can be affected by moderate amounts of alcohol in each of the following ways, EXCEPT

    A. impaired sexual performance
    B. enhanced olfactory perception
    C. a diminished sensation of cold
    D. motor skill impairment

12. Which of the following effects is MOST likely to be associated with anabolic steroid abuse?

    A. loss of appetite
    B. elevated sperm count
    C. decreased blood pressure
    D. increased levels of low-density lipoproteins (LDL) in the blood

13. "Poppers" is a slang term used to denote the inhalant

    A. amyl nitrite
    B. butane
    C. diethyl ether
    D. nitrous oxide

14. A person finds that she needs larger and larger doses of a drug to achieve intoxication or other desired effects. This person has developed

    A. psychological dependence
    B. a potentiating response
    C. a physical dependence
    D. hypersensitivity to the drug

    14._____

15. Which of the following is NOT a common side effect of antipsychotics?

    A. Dystonia
    B. Parkinsonism
    C. Impotence
    D. Cardiac arrhythmia

    15._____

16. Which of the following terms is used to denote an enhanced, unpredictable effect caused by ingesting two or more substances?

    A. Covariance
    B. Synergism
    C. Stacking
    D. Tolerance

    16._____

17. Insufflation is a technical term for the introduction of a drug by

    A. smoking
    B. suppository
    C. snorting
    D. using a skin patch

    17._____

18. One criticism of the disease model for diagnosing and treating alcoholism is that

    A. it tends to stigmatize the individual who suffers from it
    B. it is too limited and should apply to other forms of behavioral intervention
    C. it calls upon the use of public resources to treat what is essentially an individual disorder
    D. the terminology seems to discount the individual's role in the process of addiction and treatment

    18._____

19. Which of the following substances are naturally released by the brain when a person feels stress or pain?

    A. Endorphins
    B. GABA
    C. Carbon monoxide
    D. Morphine

    19._____

20. Which of the following has been identified as a factor that may significantly reduce the likelihood of drug abuse?

    A. Strong family ties
    B. High socioeconomic status
    C. Race
    D. Higher level of education completed

    20._____

21. When marijuana is smoked, it generally takes _____ for its psychoactive substance to reach the brain. 21.___

    A. a few seconds
    B. 30-45 seconds
    C. 2-3 minutes
    D. 5-8 minutes

22. Of the following processes, which produces the highest alcohol content? 22.___

    A. cold-filtering
    B. fermentation
    C. distillation
    D. brewing

23. Which of the following is a sympathomimetic effect? 23.___

    A. Constricted bronchial passages
    B. Constricted blood vessels
    C. Nausea
    D. Reduced cardiac output

24. Which of the following is an irreversible consequence of chronic alcohol abuse? 24.___

    A. Hepatitis
    B. Cirrhosis
    C. Pancreatitis
    D. Fatty liver

25. Historically, about _____ percent of heroin addicts have been able to break their addiction. 25.___

    A. 10
    B. 25
    C. 40
    D. 55

KEY (CORRECT ANSWERS)

1.	A	11.	B
2.	B	12.	D
3.	B	13.	A
4.	D	14.	C
5.	B	15.	D
6.	A	16.	B
7.	A	17.	C
8.	B	18.	D
9.	D	19.	A
10.	D	20.	A

21. A
22. C
23. B
24. B
25. A

TEST 2

DIRECTIONS: Each question or incomplete statement is followed by several suggested answers or completions. Select the one that BEST answers the question or completes the statement. *PRINT THE LETTER OF THE CORRECT ANSWER IN THE SPACE AT THE RIGHT.*

1. Typically, alcohol first produces noticeable cognitive changes at a blood alcohol concentration (BAC) of

    A. .02% to .03%
    B. .05% to .08%
    C. .10% to. 15%
    D. .16% to .20%

    1.___

2. The most common class of drugs used to treat the symptoms of those undergoing alcohol detoxification are the

    A. analgesics
    B. benzodiazepines
    C. amphetamines
    D. opiates

    2.___

3. The most common reason for young people to try illegal drugs is

    A. emotional turmoil
    B. negative reinforcement
    C. curiosity
    D. peer pressure

    3.___

4. About _____ percent of those who are classified as "heavy" marijuana users go on to use cocaine.

    A. 10
    B. 35
    C. 50
    D. 75

    4.___

5. The slang term "chronic" is used to denote a potent form of marijuana, or marijuana laced with

    A. heroin
    B. ecstasy (MDMA)
    C. cocaine
    D. LSD

    5.___

6. The ingestion of alcohol is followed by the release of _____ in the brain.
    I. dopamme
    II. serotonin
    III. norephinephrine
    IV. endorphins

    A. I and II
    B. I, II and III
    C. III and IV
    D. I, II, III and IV

    6.___

7. _____ drinking is classified as drinking up to three or four standard alcoholic drinks in a day, no more than three days a week.

   A. Social
   B. Moderate
   C. Problem
   D. Binge

7._____

8. Widespread methamphetamine abuse in the United States is generally thought to have begun in

   A. the Midwest
   B. the South
   C. the West
   D. New England

8._____

9. The term _____ is used to describe people who have both a drug problem and a psychiatric disorder.

   A. dual diagnosis
   B. compound disorder
   C. bipolar
   D. differential diagnosis

9._____

10. Which of the following common household substances can—in massive doses—cause visual and auditory hallucinations?

    A. Banana peels
    B. Nutmeg
    C. Tomatoes
    D. Ginger

10._____

11. The use of cocaine in the United States peaked between the years

    A. 1920 and 1925
    B. 1940 and 1945
    C. 1960 and 1970
    D. 1980 and 1990

11._____

12. By definition, an analgesic is a drug that is designed to

    A. relieve pain by inducing unconsciousness
    B. stimulate the central nervous system
    C. relieve pain by stimulating a natural release of endorphins
    D. relieve pain without causing a loss of consciousness

12._____

13. Creatine is most accurately classified as a(n)

    A. vitamin
    B. drug
    C. nutritional supplement
    D. steroid

13._____

14. Substances commonly considered to be "gateway" drugs include each of the following, EXCEPT

    A. nicotine
    B. caffeine
    C. marijuana
    D. alcohol

15. Which of the following inhalants are typically inhaled out of paper or plastic bags?

    A. Oxides
    B. Solvents
    C. Nitrites
    D. Ether

16. Research based on the lives of twins has suggested that the heritability of alcohol abuse is about _____ percent,

    A. 10-25
    B. 30-40
    C. 50-60
    D. 70-85

17. Each of the following drugs causes withdrawal symptoms, EXCEPT

    A. marijuana
    B. alcohol
    C. caffeine
    D. ibuprofen

18. For nearly all of the drags of abuse, the "site of action" is the

    A. central nervous system
    B. physical location where the drug enters the body
    C. particular receptor where the substance prevents or accelerates the uptake of a certain neurotransmitter
    D. peripheral nervous system

19. Which of the following neurotransmitters plays an important role in emotional, mental, and motor functions?

    A. Endorphin
    B. Glutamate
    C. Serotonin
    D. Dopamine

20. Most hallucinogenic drugs are

    A. found in the natural environment
    B. Schedule III drugs
    C. synthetics
    D. legal

21. A teenager takes some of her mother's anti-anxiety medication to contend with the stress of final examinations. This is an example of _____ use.

    A. socio-recreational
    B. experimental
    C. circumstantial-situational
    D. intensified

21.____

22. When methadone is administered to avoid the withdrawal symptoms associated with heroin, it is administered

    A. hourly
    B. twice a day
    C. daily
    D. three times a week

22.____

23. The route of administration that introduces drugs into the bloodstream the fastest is

    A. intramuscular injection
    B. snorting
    C. smoking or inhaling into lungs
    D. intravenous injection

23.____

24. A common feature of fetal alcohol syndrome is _____ deformities.

    A. digital
    B. intestinal
    C. facial
    D. cardiac

24.____

25. The part of the brain that controls the emotional response is the

    A. pons
    B. limbic system
    C. hypothalamus
    D. reticular activating system

25.____

KEY (CORRECT ANSWERS)

1. A
2. B
3. D
4. D
5. C

6. B
7. B
8. C
9. A
10. B

11. B
12. D
13. C
14. B
15. B

16. C
17. D
18. A
19. D
20. A

21. C
22. C
23. D
24. C
25. B

TEST 3

DIRECTIONS: Each question or incomplete statement is followed by several suggested answers or completions. Select the one that BEST answers the question or completes the statement. *PRINT THE LETTER OF THE CORRECT ANSWER IN THE SPACE AT THE RIGHT.*

1. Treatment for substance abuse is often considered to be a form of _____ prevention. 1.____

   A. primary
   B. secondary
   C. tertiary
   D. compound

2. Which of the following substances generally involves the LOWEST degree of physical dependence? 2.____

   A. LSD
   B. Valium
   C. Alcohol
   D. Methadone

3. Each of the following is a Schedule I drug, EXCEPT 3.____

   A. MDMA (ecstasy)
   B. GHB
   C. Cocaine
   D. LSD

4. Which of the following substances is known by the slang term "knockout drops"? 4.____

   A. Ketamine
   B. Ether
   C. Flunitrazepam (Rohypnol)
   D. Chloral hydrate

5. The most frequently committed crime in the United States is 5.____

   A. drinking underage
   B. underage purchase of alcohol
   C. driving while intoxicated
   D. illegal drug use

6. The word "psychotropic" is most accurately defined as 6.____

   A. addictive
   B. mind-altering
   C. hallucinatory
   D. mind-affecting

7. Which of the following causes of death is LEAST likely to be associated with the use of inhalants? 7.____

   A. respiratory depression
   C. cardiac arrest
   B. hypoxia
   D. aspiration of vomit

31

8. Physical dependence on a substance is indicated by the presence of

    A. denial
    B. withdrawal symptoms
    C. agonists
    D. psychological symptoms

9. Which of the following terms is used to denote the condition of a loss of contact with reality?

    A. Sociopathy
    B. Psychosis
    C. Personality disorder
    D. Neurosis

10. Which of the following is LEAST likely to be a condition that accompanies cocaine dependence?

    A. Heart failure
    B. Stroke
    C. Paranoia
    D. Irrepressible sex drive

11. More than any other drug, _____ is known for being taken in common with other recreational drugs.

    A. marijuana
    B. amphetamine
    C. ecstasy (MDMA)
    D. cocaine

12. Stage II of alcoholic withdrawal is characterized by

    A. convulsions
    B. rapid heartbeat
    C. hallucinations
    D. delirium

13. One of the earliest proponents of the therapeutic properties of cocaine was

    A. Sigmund Freud
    B. Everett Koop
    C. Timothy Leary
    D. King James I of England

14. Phencyclidine (PCP) tends to accumulate in

    A. the pancreas
    B. the liver
    C. extracellular fluid
    D. body fat

15. Which of the following neurotransmitters plays a significant role in regulating pain, eating, perception, and sleep?   15.____

    A. Dopamine
    B. Epinephrine
    C. Serotonin
    D. GABA

16. Common symptoms of marijuana use include each of the following, EXCEPT   16.____

    A. bloodshot eyes
    B. dry mouth
    C. increased intracranial pressure
    D. increased heart rate

17. Which of the following is NOT a sub-category of the class of drugs known as hallucinogens?   17.____

    A. Deliriants
    B. Psychedelics
    C. Hypnotics
    D. Dissociatives

18. Research has indicated that women who are problem drinkers   18.____

    A. have less risk for liver damage than men who are problem drinkers
    B. are at a much higher risk for osteoporosis than women who are not heavy drinkers
    C. are less likely to have an alcoholic parent than male problem drinkers
    D. are usually smokers as well

19. Of all the cases of pancreatitis that develop in the United States in a given year, about _____ % are thought to be caused by the use of alcohol.   19.____

    A. 16-25
    B. 26-35
    C. 46-55
    D. 66-75

20. Today, the most acceptable and available treatment for heroin addicts is   20.____

    A. the methadone maintenance program
    B. electroshock therapy
    C. group therapy
    D. a 12-step program similar to Alcoholics Anonymous

21. A person who is described as a compulsive drug user is likely to use drugs in order to   21.____

    A. achieve pleasure
    B. avoid discomfort
    C. satisfy curiosity
    D. fit in with peers

22. The primary ingredient in most over-the-counter stimulants is

    A. nicotine
    B. caffeine
    C. diphenhydramine
    D. amphetamine

23. The peripheral nervous system is composed of the _____ and the _____ nervous systems.

    A. somatic; autonomic
    B. limbic; spinal
    C. sympathetic; parasympathetic
    D. central; enteric

24. When snorted, cocaine takes about _____ to reach the brain.

    A. 10-15 seconds
    B. 1-5 minutes
    C. 10-15 minutes
    D. 30-45 minutes

25. Of the following, the best predictor of alcoholism is

    A. genetic predisposition
    B. level of education achieved
    C. peer pressure
    D. socioeconomic status

KEY (CORRECT ANSWERS)

1.	C	11.	C
2.	A	12.	C
3.	C	13.	A
4.	D	14.	D
5.	C	15.	C
6.	D	16.	C
7.	C	17.	C
8.	B	18.	B
9.	B	19.	D
10.	D	20.	A

21. B
22. B
23. A
24. C
25. A

TEST 4

DIRECTIONS: Each question or incomplete statement is followed by several suggested answers or completions. Select the one that BEST answers the question or completes the statement. *PRINT THE LETTER OF THE CORRECT ANSWER IN THE SPACE AT THE RIGHT.*

1. Each of the following is a risk factor that makes drug use more likely, EXCEPT

    A. a caregiver who abuses drugs
    B. poor family relations
    C. poor classroom behavior
    D. low socioeconomic status

2. The key characteristic that distinguishes hypnotic drugs from sedatives is that hypnotics are

    A. sometimes prescribed to relieve anxiety
    B. used to induce sleep
    C. prescribed to relieve pain
    D. controlled substances

3. Which of the following is NOT one of the four characteristic symptoms of addiction?

    A. Loss of control
    B. Negative consequences
    C. Compulsion to use the substance
    D. Recognition of the problem

4. The second dose or drink often does not have as great an effect as the first—an illustration of _____ tolerance.

    A. psychological   B. acute   C. behavior   D. reverse

5. One of the risks of amyl nitrite abuse is

    A. memory problems   B. flashbacks
    C. stroke   D. angina pectoris

6. The first barbiturate to be synthesized and commercially marketed was

    A. barbital   B. pento barbital
    C. secobarbital   D. methohexital

7. Which of the following drugs, first synthesized in 1874, was considered a wonder drug for the relief of pain?

    A. Aspirin   B. Laudanum   C. Cocaine   D. Heroin

8. Of the following, the class of drugs most often associated with anxiolytic (anxiety-reducing) properties is

    A. narcotics
    B. benzodiazepines
    C. hallucinogens
    D. barbiturates

9. In the United States, illicit drug use has a high correlation with

   A. depression
   B. race
   C. antisocial behavior
   D. socioeconomic status

10. A person's vital functions are regulated by the

    A. thalamus
    B. pituitary gland
    C. brain stem
    D. hippocampus

11. What is the term for a drug that is used to block the effects of narcotics?

    A. Agonist   B. Inhibitor   C. Antagonist   D. Methadone

12. A substance that reduces the effects mediated by acetylcholine in the central nervous system and the peripheral nervous system is a(n)

    A. hallucinogen
    B. benzodi azepi ne
    C. agonist
    D. anticholinergic

13. The first state to eliminate penalties for the medical use of marijuana was

    A. Alaska   B. California   C. Massachusetts   D. Oregon

14. In its effect on the central nervous system, amphetamine is very similar to

    A. marijuana   B. nicotine   C. cocaine   D. heroin

15. The psychoactive agent in glue that is sniffed or inhaled is

    A. toluene
    B. alkyl nitrite
    C. acetone
    D. xylene

16. Which of the following is a Schedule II drag?

    A. Heroin
    B. Benzodiazepines
    C. Phenobarbital
    D. Ritalin

17. At the beginning of the 21st century, alcohol was a factor in about _____ percent of traffic deaths in the United States.

    A. 20
    B. 40
    C. 60
    D. 80

18. Of the following, the stimulant most likely to be used illegally by college students in the early 21st century was

    A. cocaine
    B. methamphetamine
    C. ecstasy (MDMA)
    D. Ritalin

19. The type of drinking most often practiced by college students is _____ drinking.

    A. social
    B. binge
    C. moderate
    D. light

20. For many alcoholics, the first sign of alcohol-induced liver problems is

    A. hypertension
    B. fatty liver
    C. cirrhosis
    D. cellular edema

21. Drug addiction is typically distinguished from misuse or abuse by _____ factors.

    A. psychological
    B. criminal
    C. spiritual
    D. physical

22. Which of the following substances generally involves the HIGHEST degree of psychological dependence?

    A. Seconal
    B. Methadone
    C. LSD
    D. Methamphetamine

23. The highest rate of alcohol consumption in the United States is among

    A. adolescents
    B. young and middle-aged adults
    C. women
    D. the elderly

24. Which of the following has both hallucinogenic and anesthetic properties?

    A. Phencyclidine (PCP)
    B. Mescaline
    C. LSD
    D. Marijuana

25. At the beginning of the 21st century, the largest cocaine-producing country in the world was

    A. Colombia   B. Bolivia
    C. Mexico   D. Afghanistan

KEY (CORRECT ANSWERS)

1. D
2. B
3. D
4. B
5. C

6. A
7. D
8. B
9. C
10. C

11. C
12. D
13. B
14. C
15. A

16. D
17. B
18. D
19. B
20. B

21. D
22. D
23. B
24. A
25. A

EXAMINATION SECTION
TEST 1

DIRECTIONS: Each question or incomplete statement is followed by several suggested answers or completions. Select the one that BEST answers the question or completes the statement. *PRINT THE LETTER OF THE CORRECT ANSWER IN THE SPACE AT THE RIGHT.*

1. Research indicates that among the following psychological factors, the one most likely to increase an individual's potential for substance dependence is a(n)   1._____

    A. internal locus of control
    B. *Type A* personality
    C. high feeling of self-worth
    D. tendency toward risk-seeking behavior

2. Of the following substances, the use of_____ is most clearly linked to violent crime.   2._____

    A. marijuana
    B. alcohol
    C. LSD
    D. heroin

3. The neurotransmitter that is inhibited by sedative hypnotics is   3._____

    A. GABA
    B. dopamine
    C. acetylcholine
    D. serotonin

4. At moderate doses, stimulants can produce   4._____

    A. paranoia
    B. a sense of well-being
    C. a dreamy/sleepy state
    D. a loss of inhibitions

5. *Chipping* is a term that refers to the attempt to distribute lower doses of_____ at intervals that will avoid addiction.   5._____

    A. heroin
    B. marijuana
    C. cocaine
    D. alcohol

6. Amphetamines   6._____

    A. can cause panic, agitation, hallucinations, and paranoid delusions
    B. generally increase appetite and decrease fatigue
    C. block the reception of dopamine in the nervous system
    D. cause a period of depression and fatigue that is usually followed by feelings of euphoria

39

7. A person who is designated as a *Type 2* alcoholic has

   A. comorbid diabetes
   B. developed the disease early in life
   C. limited mobility
   D. a pronounced serotonin deficit in the brain

8. A common model of substance abuse has the person beginning with beer, wine, or cigarettes, and then moving on to hard liquor and marijuana, and subsequently to other illicit drugs. This progression is known as

   A. the tolerance curve
   B. situational use
   C. staging
   D. compulsion

9. The most appropriate goal of drug education programs is to

   A. relay information
   B. screen for likely drug users
   C. modify pre-addictive behaviors
   D. gather information from attendants

10. The primary factor in the decline in alcohol use among high school students from 1980 to the first decade of the 21st century was

    A. a trickle-down effect from the decline in alcohol use among college students
    B. a decline in binge drinking
    C. an increase in the use of illicit drugs
    D. less accessibility to alcohol

11. The most widely prescribed class of drugs in the United States is

    A. steroids
    B. barbiturates
    C. opiates
    D. benzodiazepines

12. The most likely cause of death among heavy users of alcohol is

    A. cardiovascular disease
    B. cirrhosis of the liver
    C. digestive disorders
    D. vehicular accidents

13. Cocaethylene, a dangerous drug metabolite, is produced by the combination of cocaine and

    A. alcohol
    B. heroin
    C. marijuana
    D. LSD

14. _____ is a central nervous system depressant.

    A. Heroin
    B. Marijuana
    C. Cocaine
    D. Alcohol

15. The main reason for the lengthy amount of time it takes to metabolize and excrete marijuana is that it is

    A. excreted only by the lungs
    B. stored in fat cells for up to several weeks after each use
    C. an inhaled particulate, rather than a liquid or solid
    D. one of the main components in renal calculi (kidney stones)

16. Among problem drinkers, the personality characteristic that is MOST likely to be shared is

    A. personal maladjustment
    B. depression
    C. emotional immaturity
    D. sexual dysfunction or deviance

17. Which of the following is a prominent SSRI (selective serotonin reuptake inhibitor) drug?

    A. Miltown
    B. Valium
    C. Darvon
    D. Prozac

18. Alcohol begins to influence the brain, vision, and decision-making at a blood alcohol concentration (BAC) of about

    A. 0.01
    B. 0.02
    C. 0.04
    D. 0.08

19. _____ is a term that refers to the violent behavior that results from the conflict inherent in the drug trade.

    A. Transferred intent
    B. Global wave
    C. Systemic link
    D. Collateral damage

20. The _____ theory of substance dependence holds that eventually, the vicious cycle develops in which the motivation for drug taking shifts from a desire for the euphoric high to the need to relive an increasingly intense *down* feeling that follows drug use.

    A. moral weakness
    B. circular reasoning
    C. gateway
    D. opponent-process

21. When compared to other routes of administration, drugs administered _____ are generally absorbed more slowly.

    A. by intravenous injection
    B. by intramuscular injection
    C. orally
    D. by inhalation

22. The substance _____ is used to treat overdose from heroin and other opioids by blocking the receptors that normally bind with the drug.

    A. naloxone
    B. clonidine
    C. disulfiram
    D. methadone

23. The antipsychotic drug chlorpromazine (Thorazine) is sometimes used to block the effects of each of the following, EXCEPT

    A. psilocybin
    B. mescaline
    C. PCP
    D. LSD

24. The neurotransmitter _____ is a primary agent in the *pleasure pathway* in the brain, which is believed to be involved in substance dependence.

    A. dopamine
    B. norepinephrine
    C. serotonin
    D. acetylcholine

25. Alcohol withdrawal symptoms can include
    I. convulsions
    II. insomnia
    III. tremors
    IV. hallucinations

    A. I, II and III
    B. II only
    C. II and III
    D. I, II, III and IV

KEY (CORRECT ANSWERS)

1. D
2. B
3. A
4. A
5. A

6. A
7. B
8. C
9. A
10. D

11. D
12. D
13. A
14. D
15. B

16. A
17. D
18. B
19. C
20. D

21. C
22. A
23. C
24. A
25. D

TEST 2

DIRECTIONS: Each question or incomplete statement is followed by several suggested answers or completions. Select the one that BEST answers the question or completes the statement. *PRINT THE LETTER OF THE CORRECT ANSWER IN THE SPACE AT THE RIGHT.*

1. The medical approach to alcoholism, which views it as a disease, also holds that the only acceptable goal is

    A. a lifetime prescription of Antabuse
    B. total abstinence
    C. controlled social drinking with trusted friends and family members
    D. inpatient confinement

    1.____

2. Which of the following is NOT a typical symptom of alcohol withdrawal?

    A. Sweating
    B. Irritability
    C. Flushed skin
    D. Depression

    2.____

3. In the human brain, a respiratory center necessary for breathing is located in the

    A. hindbrain
    B. cerebellum
    C. medulla
    D. thalamus

    3.____

4. _____ prevention programs are designed to prevent substance dependence before it begins.

    A. Primary
    B. Secondary
    C. Tertiary
    D. Quaternary

    4.____

5. Which of the following is NOT a synthetic opiate?

    A. Fentanyl
    B. Morphine
    C. Methadone
    D. Meperidine

    5.____

6. Benzodiazepines are prescribed primarily to treat

    A. substance dependence
    B. depression
    C. anxiety
    D. pain

    6.____

7. The area of the brain most effected by tetrahydrocannabinol (THC) is the

    A. hippocampus
    B. hypothalamus
    C. cerebrum
    D. medulla

    7.____

8. The primary feature of substance abuse is the

   A. usage of increasing amounts to achieve the same high
   B. feeling of a need for the substance
   C. use of the substance in order to prevent withdrawal
   D. continued use of a substance de spite risks or problems in living

9. Currently, methaqualone is a Schedule _____ drug.

   A. I
   B. II
   C. III
   D. IV

10. Among the elderly, the most common trigger event for excessive drinking is

    A. crime victimization
    B. retirement
    C. the death of a spouse
    D. the death of a child

11. Which of the following is a benzodiazepine?

    A. Placidyl
    B. Nembutal
    C. Valium
    D. Miltown

12. Clinically, opioids

    A. stimulate awareness
    B. have no medically recognized use
    C. increase appetite
    D. relieve pain

13. Alcoholic dementia is associated with

    A. an enlargement of the brain ventricles
    B. liver damage
    C. a permanent reduction in acetylcholine receptors
    D. a damaged hypothalamus

14. Which of the following factors is LEAST likely to result in a decrease in the intoxicating effect of a drug?

    A. concurrent intake of food
    B. increase in body fat stores
    C. greater body mass
    D. fewer body fat stores

15. Generally, the most dangerous combination of substances occurs with

    A. alcohol and marijuana
    B. alcohol and sedative hypnotics
    C. hallucinogens and narcotics
    D. amphetamines and sedative hypnotics

16. Which of the following is a risk factor for alcoholism?

    A. Not completing high school
    B. Being male
    C. Being African-American
    D. Being married

17. The route of administration that puts a drug into the layer of fat directly beneath the skin is

    A. inunction
    B. transdermal injection
    C. intramuscular injection
    D. subcutaneous injection

18. Which of the following is NOT an immediate effect of nitrous oxide?

    A. Euphoria
    B. Dehydration
    C. Cardiac arrhythmia
    D. Spontaneous laughter

19. LSD research has demonstrated that

    A. it is physiologically addictive
    B. tolerance is acquired rapidly
    C. it is absorbed slowly through the GI tract
    D. it is taken up selectively by the brain

20. In adulthood, the factor that is most closely linked to the onset of alcoholism is

    A. peer relations
    B. ethnic identity
    C. family history of alcoholism
    D. socioeconomic status

21. A primary duty of the federal Drug Enforcement Agency (DEA) is to

    A. enforce federal laws related to illicit narcotic drugs and cooperating with state and local agencies in the enforcement of state narcotics laws
    B. conduct drug abuse prevention programs
    C. gather intelligence on traffickers in illicit drugs
    D. regulate the flow and manufacture of legal but controlled drugs

22. At moderate doses, opiates can produce

   A. hypertension
   B. hypothermia
   C. respiratory depression
   D. constricted pupils

23. For most alcoholics, the first step in treatment is

   A. the first of the Twelve Steps
   B. detoxification
   C. individual therapy
   D. inpatient admission

24. *Club drugs* often used by young adults at all-night dance parties or at dance clubs and bars, include each of the following, EXCEPT

   A. ketamine
   B. GHB (gamma hydroxybutyrate)
   C. marijuana
   D. MDMA (ecstasy)

25. The most widely used opiate antagonist in withdrawal treatment is

   A. methadone
   B. clonidine
   C. chlorpromazine
   D. naltrexone

KEY (CORRECT ANSWERS)

1. B
2. C
3. C
4. A
5. B

6. C
7. A
8. D
9. A
10. C

11. C
12. D
13. A
14. D
15. B

16. B
17. D
18. B
19. B
20. C

21. D
22. B
23. B
24. C
25. D

TEST 3

DIRECTIONS: Each question or incomplete statement is followed by several suggested answers or completions. Select the one that BEST answers the question or completes the statement. *PRINT THE LETTER OF THE CORRECT ANSWER IN THE SPACE AT THE RIGHT.*

1. Which of the following sedative hypnotics is neither a barbiturate nor a benzodiazepine? 1.____

   A. Methaqualone
   B. Chlorazepate
   C. Diazepam
   D. Secobarbital

2. A substance that effectively increases the activity of a neurotransmitter by binding with a cell receptor and causing a response is known as a(n) 2.____

   A. barbiturate
   B. narcotic
   C. agonist
   D. analgesic

3. Which of the following is an opioid, developed for pharmaceutical use in the 1990s, which has proven to be addictive for many users? 3.____

   A. OxyContin
   B. Fen-Phen
   C. Tamgesic
   D. St. John's wort

4. Which of the following routes of administration greatly increases a drug user's risk for hepatitis and AIDS? 4.____

   A. Inhalation
   B. Ingestion (oral)
   C. Parenteral (injection)
   D. Topical (absorption through the skin)

5. The form of cannabis with the weakest concentration of tetrahydrocan-nabinol (THC) is 5.____

   A. marijuana
   B. sinsemilla
   C. hashish
   D. hashish oil

6. Each year, about 75 percent of the drug-related deaths in the United States are associated with 6.____

   A. alcohol
   B. polydrug episodes
   C. narcotics
   D. cocaine

48

7. The drug most often abused by adolescents is marijuana, followed by 7.____

    A. cocaine
    B. MDMA (ecstasy)
    C. barbiturates
    D. inhalants

8. What is the term for the interaction that takes place when two drugs are mixed together to produce a greater effect than that of either drug taken separately? 8.____

    A. Antagonism
    B. Potentiation
    C. Pronunciation
    D. Agonism

9. The oxidative rate-the rate at which the body metabolizes a substance-for alcohol in adults is a little under 9.____

    A. one drink per hour
    B. two drinks per hour
    C. three drinks in two hours
    D. four drinks per day

10. Which of the following is a common side effect associated with the use of antidepressant drugs, especially tricyclics (Elavil) and Serotonin and norepinephrine reuptake inhibitors (SNRIs)? 10.____

    A. Sweating
    B. Blotchy skin
    C. Constipation
    D. Ruid retention

11. _____ programs are designed to minimize the physiological changes associated with withdrawal from a substance. 11.____

    A. Withdrawal
    B. Therapeutic community
    C. 12-step
    D. Milieu

12. The most widely used sedative hypnotic drug is 12.____

    A. Seconal
    B. alcohol
    C. diazepam
    D. methaqualone

13. Of all Americans who complete a drug treatment program, the percentage who remain drug-free for at least a year afterward is about 13.____

    A. 5-10
    B. 15-35
    C. 30-50
    D. 60-80

14. *Speedball* is a street term that refers to the combination of

    A. methamphetamine and heroin
    B. cocaine and heroin
    C. cocaine and methamphetamine
    D. methamphetamine and LSD

15. Neurotransmitters are synthesized and metabolized in the body by

    A. enzymes
    B. amino acids
    C. axons
    D. metabolites

16. A substance that produces vivid sensory awareness or feelings of increased insight is said to have_____ properties.

    A. hallucinogenic
    B. psychedelic
    C. barbiturate
    D. narcotic

17. Which of the following is NOT a fundamental process associated with the concept of addiction?

    A. Reinforcement
    B. Tolerance
    C. Physical dependence
    D. Affective disorder

18. Blood alcohol concentration (BAC) becomes lethal at about

    A. 0.2
    B. 0.4
    C. 0.8
    D. 1.0

19. Which of the following is a common side effect of antipsychotic drugs?

    A. Photosensitivity
    B. Excitability
    C. Alzheimer's disease
    D. Constipation

20. Nembutal and Seconal are

    A. opiates
    B. barbiturates
    C. benzodiazepines
    D. stimulants

21. Of the following, the substance that causes the greatest overall damage to human tissue is

    A. marijuana
    B. LSD
    C. cocaine
    D. alcohol

22. Which of the following is NOT used as an alternative to anabolic steroids?

    A. Clonidine
    B. Clenbuterol
    C. GHB (gamma hydroxybutyrate)
    D. Androstenedione

23. The most likely result of drinking excessively before bedtime in order to relax is _____, which may produce anxiety and restlessness.

    A. nightmares
    B. hypertension
    C. dream deficit
    D. sleep deficit

24. Which of the following was originally used as a nasal decongestant?

    A. Cocaine
    B. Amphetamine
    C. Opium
    D. Morphine

25. The phenomenon that most clearly demonstrates that there is a cognitive as well as physiological factor involved in drug reaction and dependence is the

    A. disease model
    B. opponent-process theory
    C. expectancy effect
    D. contingency management

KEY (CORRECT ANSWERS)

1.	A	11.	A
2.	C	12.	B
3.	A	13.	C
4.	C	14.	B
5.	A	15.	A
6.	B	16.	A
7.	D	17.	D
8.	B	18.	B
9.	A	19.	A
10.	C	20.	B

21. D
22. A
23. C
24. B
25. C

TEST 4

DIRECTIONS: Each question or incomplete statement is followed by several suggested answers or completions. Select the one that BEST answers the question or completes the statement. *PRINT THE LETTER OF THE CORRECT ANSWER IN THE SPACE AT THE RIGHT.*

1. The *amotivational syndrome* is a controversial theory that refers to an indifference to long-range plans among habitual users of

    A. alcohol
    B. cocaine
    C. heroin
    D. marijuana

    1.____

2. Which of the following hallucinogens is derived from the peyote cactus?

    A. Mescaline
    B. Psilocybin
    C. Atropine
    D. Harmaline

    2.____

3. Which of the following is NOT an effect associated with the use of anabolic steroids in men?

    A. Increased sex drive
    B. Gynecomastia (breast development)
    C. Hair loss
    D. Increased blood cholesterol

    3.____

4. The most extensively used illicit drug in the United States today is

    A. marijuana
    B. amphetamine
    C. cocaine
    D. anabolic steroids

    4.____

5. The primary area of the brain that is inhibited by alcohol intoxication is the

    A. hippocampus
    B. medulla
    C. cerebrum
    D. hypothalamus

    5.____

6. Generally, the most difficult time in the process of withdrawal from heroin addiction occurs from_____ hours after the last use.

    A. 6 to 12
    B. 12 to 24
    C. 24 to 72
    D. 72 to 96

    6.____

53

7. Physical dependence on a drug is most closely associated with

   A. escalating use
   B. withdrawal symptoms
   C. missing days of work or school
   D. a strong compulsion to use the drug

8. Which of the following neurotransmitters is released at the somatic neuromuscular junctions?

   A. Dopamine
   B. Epinephrine
   C. Acetylcholine
   D. Serotonin

9. Alcohol's most significant health-related impact occurs in the_____ system.

   A. respiratory
   B. digestive
   C. endocrine
   D. central nervous

10. An effect common to the use of most inhalants is

    A. spontaneous laughter
    B. dizziness
    C. headache
    D. a loss of inhibition

11. Compared to cocaine, the stimulating effects of amphetamines are

    A. about the same in duration and intensity
    B. longer-lasting and more intense
    C. shorter-lasting and more intense
    D. longer-lasting and less intense

12. Drugs that are classified as *psychedelics* because they enhancing perceptive and thought processes of the brain include each of the following, EXCEPT

    A. LSD
    B. psilocybin
    C. mescaline
    D. ketamine

13. A disorder common among alcoholics, caused by vitamin B_1 deficiency and characterized by disorientation, confusion, abnormal eye movements, and amnesia, is_____ syndrome

    A. Ackerman's
    B. Korsakoff's
    C. Tourette's
    D. Reye's

14. The use of which of the following drugs is MOST likely to lead to tolerance or physical dependence?

    A. PCP (phencyclidine)
    B. Marijuana
    C. Amphetamine
    D. LSD

15. Common symptoms of cocaine abuse include each of the following, EXCEPT

    A. insomnia
    B. runny nose
    C. constricted pupils
    D. talkativeness

16. Available statistics on drugs and crime in the United States suggest that most narcotic addicts who commit crimes

    A. commit mostly *victimless* crimes
    B. are under the influence when they commit crimes
    C. began criminal activity after they became addicted
    D. were engaged in criminal activity before they became addicted

17. Most drugs and metabolites are excreted

    A. in the form of perspiration, saliva, and tears
    B. in the form of air expired by the lungs
    C. by the gallbladder
    D. by the kidneys

18. Which of the following drugs is used to reduce the severity of narcotic withdrawal symptoms?

    A. Clonidine
    B. Fentanyl
    C. Naltrexone
    D. Hydrocodone

19. Each of the following is a risk factor for alcohol abuse, EXCEPT

    A. peer relations
    B. a high tolerance for alcohol
    C. family relations
    D. heredity

20. By using alcohol, a person can induce an increased tolerance for Seconal, despite the fact that the user has never taken Seconal before. This is an example of

    A. distributive effect
    B. a breach in the blood-brain barrier
    C. cross-tolerance
    D. agonism

21. The class of drugs to which Ritalin belongs, and which are now the drugs of choice for treating attention-deficit/hyperactivity disorder, are

    A. stimulants
    B. depressants
    C. narcotics
    D. sedative hypnotics

21.____

22. Of the following substances, which is a narcotic?

    A. Heroin
    B. Amphetamine
    C. Alcohol
    D. LSD

22.____

23. Dexedrine and Benzedrine are commonly abused

    A. benzodiazepines
    B. amphetamines
    C. narcotics
    D. barbiturates

23.____

24. Nationwide, the primary purpose of the Drug Abuse Warning Network (DAWN) is to

    A. monitor drug-related hospital emergency department (ED) visits and drug-related deaths
    B. establish in-school programs that teach children about the consequences of drug abuse
    C. establish a network of drug treatment centers
    D. monitor the international trade in illicit drugs

24.____

25. The third stage of alcoholism, in which there is a loss of control of drinking and occasional binges of heavy drinking, is the _____ stage.

    A. pre-alcoholic
    B. chronic
    C. prodromal
    D. crucial

25.____

KEY (CORRECT ANSWERS)

1.	D	11.	D
2.	A	12.	D
3.	A	13.	B
4.	A	14.	C
5.	C	15.	C
6.	C	16.	D
7.	B	17.	D
8.	C	18.	A
9.	D	19.	B
10.	D	20.	C

21. A
22. A
23. B
24. A
25. D

EXAMINATION SECTION
TEST 1

DIRECTIONS: Each question or incomplete statement is followed by several suggested answers or completions. Select the one that BEST answers the question or completes the statement. *PRINT THE LETTER OF THE CORRECT ANSWER IN THE SPACE AT THE RIGHT.*

1. Research indicates that among all users of illicit drugs in the United States, about _____ percent use marijuana.
   - A. 35
   - B. 50
   - C. 65
   - D. 80

   1.____

2. A drug's "anxiolytic" effect refers to its ability to
   - A. relieve pain
   - B. relieve anxiety
   - C. metabolize rapidly
   - D. produce a euphoric feeling

   2.____

3. The mandrake and datura plants contain each of the following hallucinogens, EXCEPT
   - A. scopolamine
   - B. mescaline
   - C. hyoscyamine
   - D. atropine

   3.____

4. A drug dependence that results from a physician's treatment for a recognized medical condition is known as _____ addiction.
   - A. nosocomial
   - B. incidental
   - C. iatrogenic
   - D. clinical

   4.____

5. The subjective effects of barbiturates are practically indistinguishable from those of
   - A. amphetamine
   - B. alcohol
   - C. hallucinogens
   - D. benzodiazepines

   5.____

6. Home drug testing kits are typically sensitive to evidence of each of the following, EXCEPT
   - A. LSD
   - B. alcohol
   - C. amphetamine
   - D. cocaine

   6.____

7. The major portion of an alcoholic drink is metabolized by the
   - A. liver
   - B. stomach
   - C. pancreas
   - D. brain

   7.____

8. The family and friends of a person suffering from substance dependence decide to stage an intervention. Which of the following is generally believed to be a component in an effective intervention?
   - A. Convincing the substance abuser that dependence is a problem that is easily overcome.
   - B. Making a specific list of the substance abuser's transgressions over the past several months.
   - C. Focusing on all the ways in which the substance abuser is still able to function in family and society, despite his or her dependence.
   - D. Emphasizing care and concern for the substance abuser.

   8.____

9. Approximately what percentage of the antidepressants prescribed in the United States today are prescribed by physicians who are not psychiatrists?

   A. 10
   B. 33
   C. 50
   D. 75

10. Among older teenagers and young adults, one of the most powerful and consistent predictors for drug abuse is

   A. school problems
   B. personal/family crisis
   C. failed or failing relationships
   D. peer pressure

11. The greatest amount of direct societal costs, in terms of the "behavioral toxicity" of a substance, is associated in the United States with the abuse of

   A. cocaine
   B. marijuana
   C. heroin
   D. alcohol

12. Which of the following is NOT one of the classic signs of opiate overdose?

   A. Constricted pupils
   B. Coma
   C. Nausea
   D. Respiratory depression

13. The rate at which alcohol is absorbed into the bloodstream is affected by each of the following, EXCEPT the

   A. person's metabolic rate
   B. mixing of a drink with a carbonated beverage
   C. alcoholic concentration of the beverage
   D. time of day the drink is consumed

14. The rate of drug absorption is greatest in the

   A. large intestine
   B. small intestine
   C. stomach
   D. liver

15. In the human nervous system, information is transmitted outward from the nerve cell body by the

   A. mitochondrion
   B. synapse
   C. dendrite
   D. axon

16. Which of the following is NOT typically used as a "date rape" drug?

   A. Rohypnol
   B. Ketamine
   C. Ecstasy (MDMA)
   D. GHB (gamma hydroxybutyrate)

17. Which of the following is a street term for a smokeable form of amphetamine?

   A. Eight-ball
   B. Smack
   C. Ice
   D. Rock

18. The highest rate of adolescent drug use is found in

   A. the United States
   B. Thailand
   C. Russia
   D. France

19. Which of the following is a naturally occurring chemical in the brain hat has an effect similar to THC?   19._____

    A. Enkephalin B. Disulfiram
    C. GABA D. Anandamide

20. Which of the following is a synthetic opiate that is used to treat heroin withdrawal by satisfying cravings?   20._____

    A. Naloxone B. Morphine
    C. Methadone D. Disulfiram

21. Which of the following is an inhibitory neurotransmitter?   21._____

    A. GABA B. Serotonin
    C. Acetylcholine D. Norepinephrine

22. Death due to accidental overdose is MOST likely to be associated with the use of   22._____

    A. LSD B. stimulants
    C. barbiturates D. alcohol

23. Common symptoms of marijuana use include each of the following, EXCEPT   23._____

    A. talkativeness B. reddened eyes
    C. voracious appetite D. slurred speech

24. Women tend to metabolize alcohol more slowly than men because they   24._____

    A. are generally smaller in size
    B. generally have a higher percentage of body fat
    C. tend to drink more slowly
    D. usually eat more while drinking

25. Disulfiram is used as a treatment for alcoholism. It acts by   25._____

    A. blocking the reception of alcohol by brain receptors
    B. immediately breaking down alcohol into its harmless component molecules
    C. producing an immediate and severe negative reaction to alcohol intake
    D. alleviating physical withdrawal symptoms

KEY (CORRECT ANSWERS)

1. D
2. B
3. B
4. C
5. B

6. A
7. A
8. D
9. C
10. D

11. D
12. C
13. D
14. B
15. D

16. C
17. C
18. A
19. D
20. C

21. A
22. C
23. D
24. B
25. C

TEST 2

DIRECTIONS: Each question or incomplete statement is followed by several suggested answers or completions. Select the one that BEST answers the question or completes the statement. *PRINT THE LETTER OF THE CORRECT ANSWER IN THE SPACE AT THE RIGHT.*

1. The fastest growing cause of deaths related to illegal drug use today is   1.____

   A. alcohol/barbiturates overdose
   B. vehicular accidents among the intoxicated
   C. AIDS
   D. amphetamine overdose

2. During the acute phase of a person's detoxification from substance dependence, the primary focus for those who are with him/her should be to   2.____

   A. monitor physiological withdrawal symptoms and vital signs
   B. monitor for emotional outbreaks
   C. maintain wariness against manipulative or deceptive behavior
   D. arrange rehabilitation counseling

3. Among Americans, the highest rates of illicit drug use occur in the _____ age group.   3.____

   A. 11 to 18   B. 18 to 25
   C. 26 to 33   D. 34 to 41

4. For most people, signs of intoxication such as staggering, slurring of speech, or belligerence are likely to appear after about _____ alcoholic drinks.   4.____

   A. 1 or 2   B. 3 or 4
   C. 5 or 6   D. 9 or 10

5. The first federal Schedule of Controlled Substances was released in   5.____

   A. 1906   B. 1933
   C. 1970   D. 1984

6. Which of the following is a hallucinogen that is chemically similar to acetylcholine?   6.____

   A. Atropine   B. Mescaline
   C. Psilocybin   D. LSD

7. The "gateway theory" of drug use generally holds that a person's use of more dangerous illicit drugs is a predictable progression from his or her use of   7.____

   A. prescription opiates   B. marijuana
   C. inhalants   D. cocaine

8. Which of the following drugs has NOT been associated with significant physical withdrawal symptoms in users?   8.____

   A. Alcohol   B. Caffeine
   C. LSD   D. Amphetamines

9. Most drug screening programs are set up to test for   9.____

   A. the presence of drugs or metabolites in urine
   B. the presence of drugs or metabolites in blood

63

C. altered brain wave activity
D. heart arrhythmias or other irregularities

10. Common symptoms of alcohol use include each of the following, EXCEPT

    A. incoherent speech
    B. bloodshot eyes
    C. irregular walking or muscle movements
    D. heightened perception

11. In the late 20th century, federal jurisdiction for the regulation of anabolic steroids was transferred from the

    A. Drug Enforcement Agency (DEA) to the National Institutes of Health (NIH)
    B. NIH to the DEA
    C. Food and Drug Administration (FDA) to the DEA
    D. U.S. Department of Agriculture (USDA) to the FDA

12. Delirium tremens is most likely to occur in the _____ phase of alcoholism.

    A. crucial or acute
    B. chronic
    C. pre-alcoholic
    D. warning

13. The difference between the effective dose level of a drug and the lowest toxic dose is expressed as the

    A. Orange Book value
    B. margin of safety
    C. therapeutic index
    D. therapeutic equivalence

14. Generally, "moderate" drinking is defined as no more than _____ drink(s) a day for women and _____ drink(s) a day for men.

    A. 1/2; 1   B. 1; 2
    C. 2; 3   D. 2; 4

15. Studies have demonstrated a cross-tolerance between LSD and

    A. mescaline   B. MDMA (ecstasy)
    C. scopolamine   D. harmaline

16. Which of the following opiates is the most potent?

    A. Heroin   B. Morphine
    C. Fentanyl   D. Codeine

17. Naltrexone, a drug used in the treatment of alcoholism, acts by

    A. breaking alcohol down into separate molecules before it enters the bloodstream
    B. decreasing the pleasure associated with alcohol use
    C. mimicking the effects of alcohol in the brain, but with a lower intensity and duration
    D. causing the user to become ill if alcohol is ingested

18. Drug use is proportionately more common among   18._____

    A. ethnic minorities
    B. the upper class
    C. the lower classes
    D. middle-class males

19. Which of the following is an appropriate "exit result" for an abuse prevention program?   19._____

    A. A short-term effect
    B. A long-term effect
    C. A strategy for insuring and measuring success
    D. Evidence that the program is working

20. The determination of whether a person's use of a substance become "abuse" is most clearly linked to   20._____

    A. the number of times a person uses drugs in any given time period
    B. a pattern in which repeated use becomes connected to undesirable consequences
    C. the amount of the substance the user takes at any given time
    D. whether the person moves on to use illicit drugs

21. Kaposi's sarcoma is a form of cancer that has been linked to the habitual inhalation of   21._____

    A. ether
    B. nitrites
    C. petroleum distillates
    D. toluene

22. A child with one alcoholic parent has about a _____ percent chance of becoming an alcoholic him/herself.   22._____

    A. 33
    B. 50
    C. 65
    D. 80

23. The likelihood of alcohol use _____ is most likely to be determined by cultural factors.   23._____

    A. resulting in aggressive behavior
    B. reducing stress
    C. affecting the liver
    D. acting on the "pleasure pathway" of the brain

24. The substances known as endorphins, which are produced naturally in the brain and pituitary gland, are most like _____ their composition and effect.   24._____

    A. opiates
    B. stimulants
    C. barbiturates
    D. benzodiazepines

25. Schedule III drugs include   25._____
    I. anabolic steroids
    II. benzodiazepines
    III. Vicodin
    IV. morphine

    A. I only
    B. I and III
    C. II only
    D. II and IV

KEY (CORRECT ANSWERS)

1.	C	11.	C
2.	A	12.	B
3.	B	13.	B
4.	C	14.	B
5.	C	15.	A
6.	A	16.	C
7.	B	17.	B
8.	C	18.	C
9.	A	19.	A
10.	D	20.	B

21. B
22. B
23. A
24. A
25. B

TEST 3

DIRECTIONS: Each question or incomplete statement is followed by several suggested answers or completions. Select the one that BEST answers the question or completes the statement. *PRINT THE LETTER OF THE CORRECT ANSWER IN THE SPACE AT THE RIGHT.*

1. Alcohol breaks down in the body at a fairly constant rate of _____ ounce(s) per hour.   1._____
   A. 0.5 to 1.0
   B. 1.0 to 1.5
   C. 2 to 3
   D. 3 to 5

2. When the repeated intake of a substance leads to more enhanced effects, the phenomenon of sensitization, or _____, has occurred.   2._____
   A. reverse tolerance
   B. distributive effect
   C. cascading effect
   D. tolerance

3. A beverage that is "100 proof" contains _____ % alcohol   3._____
   A. 10
   B. 30
   C. 50
   D. 100

4. Marijuana is sometimes used medicinally to   4._____
   A. suppress appetite
   B. relieve intraocular (eye) pressure
   C. decrease heart rate
   D. dilate blood vessels

5. Of the following routes of administration, _____ results in the fastest delivery of a drug to the brain.   5._____
   A. ingestion
   B. inhalation
   C. topically, on the skin
   D. topically, in the eye

6. Of the following drugs, the use of _____ most commonly results in addiction.   6._____
   A. heroin
   B. methamphetamine
   C. cocaine
   D. LSD

7. The most likely reaction to the ingestion of amphetamine is   7._____
   A. loss of appetite
   B. hallucination
   C. sedation
   D. increased alertness

8. The most notorious of the "designer drugs," originally created to get around existing drug laws by modifying their molecular structures, is   8._____
   A. rohypnol
   B. ketamine
   C. psilocybin
   D. ecstasy (MDMA)

9. Naltrexone is sometimes used to treat alcoholism by

    A. reducing the craving for alcohol
    B. blocking the reception of alcohol by brain receptors
    C. reversing the effects of alcohol intoxication
    D. producing an immediate and severe negative reaction to alcohol intake

10. Of the following, which is a hallucinogen that is extremely dangerous in high doses?

    A. Phencyclidine (PCP)
    B. Mescaline
    C. Psilocybin
    D. LSD

11. "Crack" is a purified form of _____ that produces a rapid and intense reaction in the user.

    A. methamphetamine
    B. cocaine
    C. marijuana
    D. heroin

12. Which of the following hallucinogens is taken by ingesting mushrooms in which it naturally occurs?

    A. Psilocybin
    B. Mescaline
    C. LAA (lysergic acid amide)
    D. Datura

13. Which of the following approaches to drug dependence treatment is based on the idea that dependence is best treated by intensive individual and group counseling, in either a residential or non-residential setting?

    A. Therapeutic community
    B. Structural/functional
    C. Aversion therapy
    D. Medical treatment

14. Which of the following is a danger that is specific to the abuse of ether?

    A. Long-term tissue retention
    B. Powerful hallucinations
    C. Ocular damage
    D. High flammability

15. "Black tar" is a street term for an inexpensive form of

    A. heroin
    B. cocaine
    C. marijuana
    D. MDMA (ecstasy)

16. Which of the following is most often classified by itself because it is technically more than one drug, with a wide range of effects?

    A. MDMA (ecstasy)
    B. Marijuana
    C. GHB
    D. LSD

17. Drugs that are classified as Schedule II by the DEA are said to have an accepted medical use in the United States, and a high liability for abuse. Examples include each of the following, EXCEPT

    A. methadone
    B. ketamine
    C. pentobarbital
    D. diazepam

18. The Pure Food and Drug Act, which required that all drugs be accurately labeled, was passed in

    A. 1888
    B. 1906
    C. 1934
    D. 1970

19. Company-sponsored drug abuse prevention programs generally have the greatest impact on businesses in the _____ sector.

    A. transportation
    B. health care
    C. telecommunications
    D. textile

20. Which of the following is most clearly classified as a stimulant?

    A. Morphine
    B. Cocaine
    C. Alcohol
    D. Marijuana

21. The Fourth Edition of the Diagnostic and Statistical Manual of Mental Disorders-commonly known as the DSM-IV and published by the American Psychiatric Association-lists each of the following as a possible psychiatric diagnosis, EXCEPT

    A. substance dependence
    B. substance abuse
    C. alcoholism
    D. cannabis delirium

22. The primary risk associated with the medical model for managing alcohol withdrawal is

    A. the development of a dependence on a new substance
    B. seizure
    C. abnormal heart rhythm
    D. a de-emphasis on the psychological factors that led to abuse

23. _____ prevention programs are aimed at people who have tried a certain drug or other drugs, but have not been treated for dependence

    A. Primary
    B. Secondary
    C. Tertiary
    D. Quaternary

24. Most of the money-from all sources-used in the United States to fight the problem of substance abuse is allocated to

    A. reducing the supply
    B. treatment programs
    C. law enforcement
    D. prevention programs

25. Alcohol contains
   I. vitamins
   II. calories
   III. minerals
   IV. proteins

   A. I and II
   B. II only
   C. I and III
   D. I, II, III and IV

KEY (CORRECT ANSWERS)

1.	A	11.	B
2.	A	12.	A
3.	C	13.	A
4.	B	14.	D
5.	B	15.	A
6.	A	16.	B
7.	D	17.	D
8.	D	18.	B
9.	A	19.	A
10.	A	20.	B

21. C
22. A
23. B
24. C
25. B

TEST 4

DIRECTIONS: Each question or incomplete statement is followed by several suggested answers or completions. Select the one that BEST answers the question or completes the statement. *PRINT THE LETTER OF THE CORRECT ANSWER IN THE SPACE AT THE RIGHT.*

1. E.M. Jellinek's theory of alcoholism was that it was a(n)

    A. form of neurosis
    B. progressive disease that moved through several predictable stages
    C. form of deviance similar to other forms of insanity
    D. condition that arose directly as a result of one's home environment

2. The lifetime prevalence of alcohol dependence (the percentage of people who are alcoholics at any point in their lives) in the United States is about _____ percent.

    A. 6
    B. 12
    C. 18
    D. 25

3. Which of the following is NOT likely to be caused by chronic marijuana use?

    A. Impaired ability to learn
    B. Diminished motivation to work
    C. Aggressive behavior
    D. Decreased testosterone levels in men

4. "Hallucinogenic persisting perceptive disorder" is a clinical term for

    A. Formication
    B. Eye twitches
    C. Flashback
    D. Euphoria

5. Cocaine works by increasing the availability of _____ in the brain.

    A. acetylcholine
    B. serotonin
    C. epinephrine
    D. dopamine

6. Another term by which the opioid drugs are known is

    A. sedatives
    B. barbiturates
    C. hypnotics
    D. narcotics

7. Of the following substances, which is classified as both a hallucinogen and a stimulant?

    A. Cocaine
    B. Ecstasy (MDMA)
    C. Heroin
    D. Mescaline

8. In the year _____, the federal Food and Drug Administration began to require that new drugs had to be demonstrated to be effective before they could be marketed.

    A. 1906
    B. 1912
    C. 1962
    D. 1970

9. Accepted therapeutic uses of opiates include each of the following, EXCEPT

    A. cough suppression
    B. treatment of liver insufficiency
    C. treatment of severe diarrhea
    D. pain relief

10. Symptoms associated with heroin withdrawal include each of the following, EXCEPT

   A. muscle and bone pain
   B. vomiting
   C. cold sweats
   D. abdominal cramps

11. A drug introduced through IM injection will be absorbed most rapidly if injected into the

   A. deltoid   B. abdominals
   C. quadriceps   D. gluteals

12. When two drugs are present in the system at one time, but the effect of one reduces or blocks the effect of the other, it is said to have a(n) _____ effect.

   A. potentiating   B. withdrawal
   C. inhibiting   D. synergistic

13. A(n) _____ prevention program is oriented to those who have already been treated for substance abuse.

   A. primary   B. secondary
   C. tertiary   D. outpatient

14. Increased heart rate and blood pressure as the result of taking a drug are examples of _____ activation.

   A. somatic   B. peripheral
   C. parasympathetic D. sympathetic

15. Mescaline and psilocybin belong to the _____ class of drugs.

   A. hallucinogen   B. narcotic
   C. stimulant   D. depressant

16. The primary behavioral consequences of marijuana use are associated with

   A. problem-solving
   B. impulse control
   C. memory and attention
   D. sleep and dreams

17. The "flushing syndrome" associated with alcohol use typically involves each of the following symptoms, EXCEPT

   A. memory problems
   B. hives
   C. headache
   D. rapid heart rate

18. Deliriant, or anticholinergic, drugs include

   A. ketamine   B. nitrous oxide
   C. datura   D. psilocybin

19. "Distilled spirits" or "hard liquor" generally has an alcohol content of about _____ percent

    A. 3.2 to 12.0
    B. 15 to 30
    C. 40 to 50
    D. 60 to 80

20. Which of the following is generally NOT an effect of chronic marijuana use?

    A. Lower infant birth weight
    B. Lower fertility for women
    C. Damage to the respiratory system
    D. Lowered sperm count in men

21. Currently, the preferred confirmatory test for the presence of alcohol and drugs is

    A. spectrophotometry
    B. radioimmunoassay
    C. gas chromatography/mass spectrometry (GC/MS)
    D. thin layer chromatography

22. Which of the following is a term for the state arising from alcohol abuse in which a person has difficulties in problem-solving, organizing facts about one's identity and environment, and remembering information?

    A. Alcoholic dementia
    B. Potentiation
    C. Alcoholic cirrhosis
    D. Alcoholic aphasia

23. Feelings of euphoria associated with the use of most inhalants tend to last about

    A. 40 seconds
    B. 10 minutes
    C. one hour
    D. 4 hours

24. A habitual marijuana user has discovered that he needs to smoke three times as much to achieve the level of intoxication he achieved a year ago.
    This phenomenon is known as

    A. withdrawal
    B. potentiation
    C. reversion
    D. tolerance

25. Drugs that are classified as Schedule I by the DEA are said to have no accepted medical use in the United States, and have a high liability for abuse. Examples of Schedule I drugs include each of the following, EXCEPT

    A. marijuana
    B. mescaline
    C. morphine
    D. heroin

KEY (CORRECT ANSWERS)

1. B
2. B
3. C
4. C
5. D

6. D
7. B
8. C
9. B
10. D

11. A
12. C
13. C
14. D
15. A

16. C
17. A
18. C
19. C
20. B

21. C
22. A
23. C
24. D
25. C

EXAMINATION SECTION
TEST 1

DIRECTIONS: Each question or incomplete statement is followed by several suggested answers or completions. Select the one that BEST answers the question or completes the statement. *PRINT THE LETTER OF THE CORRECT ANSWER IN THE SPACE AT THE RIGHT.*

1. Methadone is a synthetic substitute for

    A. demerol
    B. morphine
    C. laudanum
    D. pentothal

    1._____

2. A family of synthetic drugs made from coal tar is the

    A. opiates
    B. cocaines
    C. bromides
    D. barbiturates

    2._____

3. A drug which does NOT cause physical addiction or withdrawal symptoms but is regulated by the government as a narcotic is

    A. codeine
    B. morphine
    C. cocaine
    D. heroin

    3._____

4. The term *tracks* is associated with the users of

    A. L.S.D.
    B. red devils
    C. methadone
    D. heroin

    4._____

5. Of the following drugs, the one that is a stimulant is

    A. alcohol
    B. amphetamines
    C. barbiturates
    D. opiates

    5._____

6. Amytal, Seconal and Nembutal are prescription drugs classified as

    A. barbiturates
    B. hallucinogens
    C. opiates
    D. amphetamines

    6._____

7. A drug which is classed legally as a narcotic while medically it is NOT is

    A. opium
    B. cocaine
    C. heroin
    D. codeine

    7._____

8. Of the following regarding barbiturates, the INCORRECT statement is:

    A. More people die as a result of acute intoxication from barbiturates than from any other drug poisoning
    B. Taking barbiturates along with alcoholic beverages may prove to be fatal
    C. The medicinal use of barbiturates has been prescribed for sedation, sleep-producing, epilepsy, and high blood pressure
    D. Barbiturates are not depressants

    8._____

9. The CORRECT association related to the special language of drug users is

    A. candy–hallucinogens
    B. cartwheels–tranquilizers
    C. bennies–barbiturates
    D. co-pilots–amphetamines

    9._____

10. As related to treatment and rehabilitation of drug abuse, the CORRECT association is

    A. detoxification—substituting a less harmful drug
    B. maintenance—peer group support
    C. encounter therapy—in-patient hospitalization
    D. therapeutic community—halfway house using former addicts

11. Methaqualone is used medically as a

    A. safe substitute for barbiturates
    B. non-addicting anti-convulsant
    C. prescription for sleeplessness
    D. prevention of skeletal abnormalities in human fetuses

12. All of the following statements concerning the intake of alcohol in the body are correct EXCEPT:

    A. Although alcohol has a caloric content, it is expended instead of being stored in the body.
    B. A small percentage of the alcohol taken into the body is eliminated through the lungs.
    C. Alcohol produces a feeling of warmth with an actual lowering of body temperature.
    D. Digestive changes are necessary before alcohol can be absorbed from the stomach.

13. All of the following characteristics predispose a person to alcoholism EXCEPT having

    A. little tolerance for frustration
    B. low energy levels and strong impulse control
    C. strong feelings of alienation
    D. conflicts in family relationships

14. The MOST effective approach for a teacher to use in an alcohol education unit is to

    A. stress the evils of alcoholism
    B. emphasize the importance of the freedom of the individual to make responsible choices
    C. present facts about alcohol to the students
    D. use the scare approach to discourage students from using alcohol

15. In developing a program of treatment of the alcoholic, the LEAST important consideration is

    A. hospitalization until completion of the treatment
    B. detoxification
    C. physical rehabilitation including nutritional assistance
    D. maintenance of abstinence

16. One of the EARLIEST effects of alcohol on the body is

    A. reduced heart action
    B. loss of equilibrium
    C. decrease in judgment and self-control
    D. blurred and double vision

17. It is CORRECT to state that the *immediate* effect of alcohol on the body is to   17.____

    A. constrict surface blood vessels
    B. decrease the rate of the heartbeat
    C. increase blood pressure
    D. decrease body temperature

18. Of the following concerning alcohol, the CORRECT statement is: 18.____

    A. Alcohol acts principally on the central nervous system
    B. As a rule, black coffee will do away with intoxication
    C. There are no individual differences among people which relate to alcoholism
    D. About 50% of the alcohol consumed is eliminated unchanged through the kidneys and lungs

19. As alcohol is oxidized in the body tissues, the energy it contains is   19.____

    A. used up in muscular activity
    B. used in accelerated activity of the nervous system
    C. stored in the body
    D. given off as heat

20. Of the following, the substance with addicting properties would be   20.____

    A. mescaline   B. phenobarbital
    C. librium   D. cocaine

21. When considered as a drug, the MOST accurate classification which describes alcohol is that it is a   21.____

    A. stimulant   B. depressant
    C. hallucinogen   D. tranquilizer

22. The MOST common signs and symptoms associated with the use of marijuana are   22.____

    A. thirst, drowsiness, and passiveness
    B. pink eyes, increased pulse rate, and hunger
    C. discomfort, anxiety, and general ataxia
    D. increased libido, decreased blood pressure, and pupil dilation

23. While under the influence of morphine, an addict will *usually*   23.____

    A. experience an abnormal dryness of the nose
    B. have contracted, pinpoint pupils of the eyes
    C. feel strong and superior and experience loss of fatigue
    D. be very talkative and will not listen to others

24. Of the following statements concerning drugs, the CORRECT one is: 24.____

    A. As a person's tolerance to barbiturates increases, his tolerance level to other drugs also increases.
    B. Many heroin addicts will use amphetamines when they cannot obtain heroin.
    C. Most experts consider barbiturate addiction more dangerous than heroin addiction.
    D. When skin popping, the user will most often inject directly into a vein.

25. The time between the consuming of alcohol and its beginning to be absorbed into the bloodstream may be *as little as* _____ minutes.

    A. 2 B. 5 C. 8 D. 10

26. All of the following statements concerning alcohol and its effect on the body are correct EXCEPT:

    A. The constant presence of alcohol impairs the liver cells in their ability to store glycogen
    B. At high concentrations, alcohol causes the lessening of gastric juice secretion
    C. Beriberi is one of the commonest deficiency diseases associated with alcoholism
    D. Alcohol increases the enzyme action in the stomach

27. The MOST severe withdrawal reactions result from addiction to

    A. cocaine B. heroin
    C. barbiturates D. mescaline

28. The difference between marijuana and heroin is that

    A. marijuana has no proven medical use
    B. heroin is more addictive
    C. pure heroin is better to use than pure marijuana
    D. the emotions are more directly affected by marijuana than by heroin

29. With regard to marijuana, the CORRECT statement is:

    A. More severe penalties will decrease the problem.
    B. Marijuana use usually leads to heroin use.
    C. Marijuana is harmless.
    D. Driving under the influence of marijuana is hazardous.

30. Of the following statements, it is TRUE to say that marijuana

    A. is an aphrodisiac
    B. is addictive
    C. interferes with the thought processes
    D. causes violence and crime

31. The MOST widely misused of all drugs is

    A. alcohol B. marijuana
    C. heroin D. cocaine

32. All of the following concerning heroin are correct EXCEPT it

    A. is an antispasmodic
    B. is a derivative of opium
    C. is considered a hypnotic rather than a narcotic
    D. has mild, pain relieving powers

33. All of the following associations are correct EXCEPT

   A. narcotic–novocaine
   B. barbiturate–luminal
   C. stimulant–amphetamine
   D. sedative–benzedrine

34. Alcohol supplies to the body

   A. minerals
   B. protein
   C. calories
   D. none of these

35. All of the following statements concerning alcohol are correct EXCEPT:

   A. The effects of alcohol upon the brain are not felt until the alcohol begins to get into the bloodstream.
   B. While alcohol is absorbed quickly by the body, it is eliminated slowly.
   C. The metabolism of alcohol in the body is speeded up by increased activity.
   D. The stomach cannot change alcohol.

KEY (CORRECT ANSWERS)

1.	B	11.	C	21.	B
2.	C	12.	D	22.	B
3.	C	13.	B	23.	B
4.	D	14.	B	24.	C
5.	B	15.	A	25.	A
6.	A	16.	C	26.	B
7.	B	17.	D	27.	C
8.	D	18.	A	28.	B
9.	D	19.	D	29.	D
10.	B	20.	C	30.	C

31. A
32. C
33. D
34. C
35. C

EXAMINATION SECTION
TEST 1

DIRECTIONS: Each question or incomplete statement is followed by several suggested answers or completions. Select the one that BEST answers the question or completes the statement. *PRINT THE LETTER OF THE CORRECT ANSWER IN THE SPACE AT THE RIGHT.*

1. The fact is that alcohol

    A. stimulates driving alertness when sleep is needed
    B. is a depressant
    C. has no caloric value
    D. affects all persons in the same degree

2. The fallacy is that alcohol

    A. slows reaction time
    B. has no mineral value
    C. is an anesthetic
    D. cures a cold

3. The CORRECT regimen for an alcoholic is to

    A. drink less gradually
    B. drink just before meals
    C. stop drinking alcohol beverages completely
    D. drink only at home

4. In the brain, excessive alcohol acts as a(n)

    A. stimulant
    B. anaesthetic
    C. readily available fuel
    D. vitamin-carrier

5. The trend toward alcoholism is MOST often

    A. a symptom of personality maladjustment
    B. caused by heredity
    C. associated with the sex of the individual
    D. associated with the individual's occupation

6. Excessive intake of alcoholic beverages over a period of time

    A. hampers the production of gastric juice
    B. reduces nervous anxiety
    C. increases mental alertness
    D. dilates the blood vessels

1._____

2._____

3._____

4._____

5._____

6._____

7. Today, the nature of general clinical treatment of alcoholism is

   A. group psychotherapy
   B. incarceration
   C. tapering off and substitution
   D. physiotherapy

8. An ounce of alcohol (95%) has an APPROXIMATE caloric value of

   A. 200   B. 300   C. 400   D. 500

9. *Alcoholics Anonymous* was organized by

   A. alcoholic addicts
   B. the federal government
   C. private organizations
   D. the American Medical Association

10. It is believed that atabuse

    A. sensitizes humans against alcohol
    B. forms an unstable compound with alcohol
    C. stimulates the gag reflex
    D. promotes elimination of alcohol from the body

11. Excessive alcohol intake ultimately

    A. stimulates body reactions
    B. accelerates mental alertness
    C. depresses
    D. lowers body resistance to infections

12. The malnutrition associated with alcoholism USUALLY results from

    A. impaired digestion
    B. disturbed metabolism
    C. excessive craving for proteins
    D. reduction in diet essentials

13. Excessive use of alcohol is indulged in because it is believed to

    A. quiet the nerves
    B. stimulate brain action
    C. relieve emotional tension
    D. overcome social inadequacy

14. Alcohol FIRST affects

    A. judgment   B. memory
    C. muscular coordination D. control of speech

15. To the nervous system, alcohol acts as a

 A. stimulant B. depressant
 C. gratifier D. agitator

15.____

16. Characteristic symptoms of chronic alcoholism include

 A. damage to brain tissue
 B. increase in weight
 C. exsiccosis
 D. periods of depression

16.____

17. The anesthetizing action of alcohol FIRST affects the exercise of

 A. muscular coordination B. control of speech
 C. judgment D. memory

17.____

18. Acute intoxication may properly be labeled a psychosis because it involves

 A. severe loss of contact with reality
 B. emotional inadequacies
 C. intellectual limitations
 D. bodily as well as mental disease

18.____

19. The treatment of alcoholic pellagra is a balanced diet AND

 A. penicillin injections
 B. oral antibiotics
 C. thiamin injections
 D. amytal injections

19.____

20. *Cured* alcoholics

 A. can control the amount they drink
 B. cannot ever *drink normally*
 C. need moral help to drink within *normal limits*
 D. can drink some alcohol as long as they eat with it

20.____

21. Alcohol is MOST often used excessively in order to

 A. induce sleep
 B. stimulate brain action
 C. overcome social inadequacy
 D. furnish temporary release from tensions

21.____

22. To cure drug addiction, the A.M.A. believes that the BEST procedure is to

 A. maintain stable dosages in addicts
 B. furnish narcotics at no cost
 C. establish withdrawal clinics
 D. give constant control in a drug–free environment

22.____

23. Of the following, the MOST dangerous of the narcotic poisons is 23.___
   A. codeine   B. opium   C. heroin   D. marijuana

24. Statistics indicate that MOST youngsters start the drug habit with 24.___
   A. marijuana   B. heroin   C. cocaine   D. morphine

25. Alcohol is a 25.___
   A. stimulant   B. narcotic   C. depressant   D. none of these

KEY (CORRECT ANSWERS)

1. B		11. C	
2. D		12. D	
3. C		13. C	
4. B		14. A	
5. A		15. B	
6. A		16. D	
7. A		17. C	
8. A		18. A	
9. A		19. C	
10. A		20. B	

21. D
22. D
23. C
24. A
25. C

TEST 2

DIRECTIONS: Each question or incomplete statement is followed by several suggested answers or completions. Select the one that BEST answers the question or completes the statement. *PRINT THE LETTER OF THE CORRECT ANSWER IN THE SPACE AT THE RIGHT.*

1. In general, of the following, the MOST effective cure of addiction to drugs is   1._____

   A. sustained medical treatment
   B. change of occupation
   C. voluntary tapering off of the use of drugs
   D. conquering the habit by will power

2. The method used to train teenagers in the control of narcotic habits in a school on Ward's Island is the   2._____

   A. penal colony
   B. strict regulatory
   C. clinical examination control
   D. permissive

3. A drug which is a substitute for morphine in the treatment of drug addiction is   3._____

   A. codeine   B. demerol   C. pantapon   D. methadone

4. An hypnotic drug which does NOT initiate drug addiction is   4._____

   A. dormison   B. sodium amytal
   C. sodium phenobarbital D. seconal

5. The MOST harmful drug derived from opium is   5._____

   A. heroin   B. morphine   C. cocaine   D. codeine

6. The MOST recent statistics indicate that, of the following, the leading cause of accidental deaths from poisoning is   6._____

   A. morphine   B. narcotine
   C. barbituates   D. lead

7. Marijuana is made from   7._____

   A. opium   B. codeine
   C. hemp leaves D. cocoa

8. To a drug addict, reefer or joint mean   8._____

   A. cigarettes   B. powders
   C. capsules   D. pills

9. *Goofballs* used by drug addicts contained   9._____

   A. chloral   B. hyoscyamine
   C. stramonium   D. barbituric acid

10. Recent statistics indicate that MOST youngsters start the drug habit with   10._____

    A. marijuana   B. heroin   C. cocaine   D. morphine

11. Recent information regarding cocaine indicates that it

    A. is purely recreational
    B. is highly addictive
    C. is helpful in reducing stress and hypertension
    D. should be used only prescribed by a physician

12. A habit-forming drug is

    A. sulfathiozole   B. quinidine
    C. demerol   D. potassium acetate

13. Usually, the FIRST step to drugs by a youngster is a

    A. deck   B. snort   C. reefer   D. cap

14. Preventing unlawful trade in narcotics is assigned to

    A. Drug Authority
    B. Bureau of Narcotics
    C. Bureau of Customs
    D. United Nations Commission on Narcotic Drugs

15. *Tolerance* in drug addiction means the amount that

    A. quiets the nerves
    B. produces unconsciousness
    C. can be taken without character changes
    D. produces the desired effect

16. Marijuana is obtained from the

    A. hemp plant   B. thorn apple
    C. cocoa shrub   D. nightshade plant

17. According to the authorities, relationship between the incidence of cancer and smoking is

    A. controversial   B. negative
    C. positive   D. incidental

18. The responsibility for preventing unlawful domestic trade in narcotics rests with the

    A. United Nations Commission on Narcotics
    B. Bureau of Customs, U.S. Treasury Department
    C. Drug Enforcement Agency (DEA), U.S. Treasury Department
    D. United States Drug Authority, Legal Division

19. In addicts, drug withdrawal symptoms include vomiting and changes in

    A. A. pupils of the eyes
    B. muscular control
    C. color of the skin
    D. color of the whites of the eyeballs

20. If a teacher discovers a pupil who is taking drugs, she should report it to the

    A. dean or assistant principal
    B. police
    C. principal of the school
    D. pupil's parents

20._____

21. In addicts, a moderate drug abstinence syndrome is characterized by

    A. fever, increased blood pressure, insominia, acute restlessness, and rapid breathing
    B. depression, excessive perspiration, and yawning
    C. inertia, body tremors, and fits of sneezing
    D. diarrhea, chills, and depression

21._____

22. Opium is derived from

    A. hemp fiber   B. nightshade plant
    C. poppy   D. ragweed

22._____

23. A *mainliner* is a drug addict who uses the drug for

    A. intra-muscular injection
    B. snorting
    C. smoking
    D. intra-venal injection

23._____

24. Prolonged administration of narcotics is MOST likely to result in

    A. addiction
    B. reduced physical resistance
    C. increased aggressiveness
    D. need for a change in prescription

24._____

25. A plant from which peyote is obtained is the

    A. nightshade plant   B. fox glove
    C. gentian   D. mescal catcus

25._____

26. *Half-way house* is the name of a(n)

    A. dual purpose house providing facilities for living as well as conducting a business
    B. nursing home for terminal care of cancer patients
    C. rehabilitation center for ex-drug addicts and patients released from mental hospitals
    D. nursing home for senile aged persons

26._____

27. To avoid detection, the heroin addict injects the 27.____

   A. nasal mucosa and the gums
   B. gums and the vagina
   C. nasal mucosa and the vagina
   D. conjunctiva

28. A highly dangerous and addictive synthetic narcotic is 28.____

   A. amidol
   B. amidone
   C. cobalamine
   D. pyridoxine

29. During the 1993-1997 term of President Clinton, drug use by young people 29.____

   A. remained steady
   B. increased by one million
   C. declined
   D. cannot be statistically determined

30. A POSITIVE effect of decriminalizing drug use by medical administration would be 30.____

   A. fewer addicts
   B. increased medical costs
   C. less drug-related crime
   D. making drug use more acceptable

KEY (CORRECT ANSWERS)

1.	A	11.	B	21.	A
2.	D	12.	C	22.	C
3.	D	13.	C	23.	D
4.	A	14.	B	24.	A
5.	A	15.	D	25.	D
6.	C	16.	A	26.	C
7.	C	17.	C	27.	B
8.	A	18.	C	28.	B
9.	D	19.	A	29.	B
10.	A	20.	C	30.	C

EXAMINATION SECTION
TEST 1

DIRECTIONS: Each question or incomplete statement is followed by several suggested answers or completions. Select the one that BEST answers the question or completes the statement. *PRINT THE LETTER OF THE CORRECT ANSWER IN THE SPACE AT THE RIGHT.*

1. Which of the following is NOT an inherent characteristic of addiction? 1.____

    A. Tolerance changes
    B. Dissolution of relationships
    C. Physiological dependence
    D. Loss of self-control

2. Which type of factor in an individual's predisposition to addiction has the GREATEST potential to increase the risk of addiction after exposure to a substance? 2.____

    A. Genetic   B. Constitutional   C. Psychological   D. Sociocultural

3. The enabling behavior MOST likely practiced by the addicted person's family members in the early stages of addiction are 3.____

    A. cooperation and collaboration
    B. protecting and shielding
    C. codependence and cohabitation
    D. control and guilt

4. When making initial inquiries about an addicted person's drug or alcohol abuse patterns and history, which of the following is probably the LEAST reliable? 4.____

    A. Information provided by the subject's friends and relatives
    B. Information provided by the patient or subject
    C. Medical histories of subject's family members
    D. Subject's medical record

5. Which of the following is NOT one of the physical factors influencing addiction? 5.____

    A. Heredity
    B. Brain chemistry
    C. Metabolism
    D. Race

6. In a recovery treatment center, which of the following behaviors or characteristics gives the STRONGEST indication that a subject is still addicted? 6.____

    A. Feeling caged or jailed
    B. Mood swings
    C. Nervousness
    D. Depression

7. Which of the following is NOT true of *leverages* used by members of an intervention team to induce an addicted person to voluntarily submit to treatment? They should 7.____

    A. only be used as a last resort
    B. not be carried out if they will result in isolating the addicted person
    C. be agreed upon and supported by every member of the intervention team
    D. not be threatened unless they will definitely be implemented

8. What percentage of untreated alcoholics will eventually experience seizures?

   A. 5-15% B. 20-30% C. 40-50% D. 55-75%

9. Which of the following is a sign that an adolescent has entered the late stages of addiction?

   A. Impulsiveness
   B. Decrease in attention span
   C. Chronic depression
   D. Denial

10. The type of drug dependency requiring the longest treatment time is USUALLY caused by

    A. alcohol
    B. amphetamines
    C. opiates or cocaine
    D. hallucinogens

11. Which of the following is NOT one of the primary factors in the formula that results in addiction?

    A. Drug effect
    B. Social constraints
    C. Predisposition for abuse
    D. Enabling factors

12. Drugs sometimes used in detoxification and which occupy a person's opiate-receptor sites without creating an accompanying sense of euphoria or loss of consciousness are

    A. opioids
    B. opiates
    C. agonists
    D. placebos

13. The normalization process during the late recovery phase of treatment includes

    A. increasingly sobriety-centered lifestyle
    B. discussion of drug hunger
    C. personality growth
    D. stress reduction techniques

14. Which of the following unconscious defense mechanisms, used by an addicted person, is characterized by partial awareness of the severity of the addiction?

    A. Denial
    B. Minimization
    C. Rationalization
    D. Isolation

15. The characteristic of an addicted person's recovery illustrated by the person's attempt to repair the relationships damaged by his/her addiction is

    A. fellowship
    B. surrender
    C. admission
    D. restitution

16. Which of the following is a sign that a drinker has entered the late stages of alcoholism?

    A. Progressive increase in drinking
    B. Broken promises to friends and family
    C. Personality changes
    D. Malnutrition

17. An alcoholic subject is said to have entered stage four of the withdrawal process if he or she experiences

    A. seizures
    B. delirium tremens
    C. vomiting
    D. hallucinations

18. Which of the following unconscious defense mechanisms, used by an addicted person, is characterized by an avoidance of feelings through focusing on logic?

    A. Rationalization
    B. Intellectualization
    C. Repression
    D. Projection

19. Measuring from the starting point of detoxification, what is typically the amount of time required for a recovering person to regain the level of health and well-being associated with his/her pre-addiction lifestyle?

    A. 6 months   B. 1 year   C. 18 months   D. 3 years

20. A characteristic that typically differentiates teenage alcoholism from adult alcoholism is that teenagers

    A. are more likely to explain that they drink to celebrate or be sociable
    B. have a more difficult time with recovery
    C. claim drinking as an escape from life's problems
    D. sustain less physiological damage

21. Which type of recovery treatment is reserved for the most advanced cases of addiction?

    A. Day treatment
    B. Residential treatment
    C. Inpatient hospitalization
    D. Partial hospitalization

22. The use of which opiate drug typically carries the LOWEST risk for dependency or abuse?

    A. Percodan   B. Methadone   C. Codeine   D. Demerol

23. What is the APPROXIMATE mortality rate for alcoholic patients who suffer from delirium tremens?

    A. Zero   B. 1-10%   C. 10-20%   D. 20-30%

24. Addiction is a process influenced primarily by each of the following EXCEPT

    A. factors relating to the individual user
    B. various social factors
    C. factors relating to specific physiological health concerns
    D. factors relating to the drug being used

25. Which of the following statements about alcoholism is NOT true?

    A. Children of alcoholics often learn alcoholic behavior from their parents.
    B. Divorce, loss of a job, death of a loved one, and other life traumas can cause alcoholism.
    C. Alcoholism is often a symptom of larger psychological problems.
    D. An alcoholic in the throes of the disease drinks to avoid self-destruction.

KEY (CORRECT ANSWERS)

1. B
2. A
3. B
4. B
5. D

6. A
7. B
8. A
9. C
10. C

11. B
12. C
13. C
14. B
15. D

16. D
17. B
18. B
19. C
20. A

21. C
22. C
23. C
24. C
25. D

TEST 2

DIRECTIONS: Each question or incomplete statement is followed by several suggested answers or completions. Select the one that BEST answers the question or completes the statement. *PRINT THE LETTER OF THE CORRECT ANSWER IN THE SPACE AT THE RIGHT.*

1. Age, peers, and status are examples of _____ factors in an individual's predisposition to addiction.

    A. genetic   B. constitutional   C. psychological   D. sociocultural

2. How many days should an alcoholic subject's detoxification process typically last?

    A. 1-10   B. 10-20   C. 20-30   D. 30-40

3. Which of the following is NOT true of the confrontation that takes place between members of an intervention team and an addicted person?
It must

    A. be rehearsed by all team members together
    B. involve quick-thinking people who can formulate responses to unanticipated statements
    C. involve people from a variety of the addicted person's life experiences
    D. be rigidly planned and structured

4. What is the characteristic of an addicted person's recovery illustrated by the person's expression of willingness to accept the help of treatment staff in the recovery process?

    A. Surrender   B. Acceptance   C. Fellowship   D. Restitution

5. In the early stages of an addicted or alcoholic person's recovery, the process of nutritional repair should include each of the following EXCEPT

    A. three good meals a day
    B. total elimination of caffeine intake
    C. three nutritious snacks a day
    D. increasing the amount of sugars in the diet

6. Which of the following stages in the progression to freedom from addiction is considered to be the final stage, at which recovery is complete?

    A. Spiritual well-being   B. Mental well-being
    C. Total abstinence   D. Physical well-being

7. The FIRST goal of recovery treatment is to remedy _____ damage to the addicted person.

    A. social   B. psychological   C. physical   D. spiritual

8. Which of the following steps should be taken LAST by friends/family members who want to practice intervention in a person's addiction?

    A. Devising a treatment plan
    B. Confronting the addicted person
    C. Getting help for the person's family
    D. Asking others for help

93

9. Each of the following is a disadvantage associated with the use of sedatives during an alcoholic subject's withdrawal EXCEPT that it

    A. increases suspicion and paranoia
    B. conflicts with the *abstinence* goal of detoxification
    C. lengthens the detoxification period
    D. interferes with the subject's alertness and early participation in treatment

10. Which of the following symptoms does addiction MOST commonly share with other chronic, debilitating diseases?

    A. Central nervous system damage
    B. Seizures
    C. Denial
    D. Physiological damage

11. An addicted person who would require one of the more intense levels of recovery treatment and care would PROBABLY have

    A. minor withdrawal symptoms
    B. family members who attend Al-Anon
    C. already be resigned to treatment
    D. already attempted recovery at least once and failed

12. The enabling behavior MOST likely practiced by the addicted person's family members in the advanced stages of addiction is

    A. cooperation   B. protecting
    C. codependence   D. guilt

13. Which of the following is NOT a symptom associated with stage two in an alcoholic subject's withdrawal process?

    A. Rapid heartbeat   B. Hand tremors
    C. Insomnia   D. Seizures

14. During intervention, participants on the intervention team should avoid describing to the addicted person

    A. concerns for the addicted person's health
    B. observed examples of addiction-related incidents
    C. observed consequences of addiction-related incidents
    D. personal assessment of emotional damage inflicted upon the addicted person's relations

15. During recovery, a subject sometimes becomes dependent on a drug that has the same relative effects on the central nervous system as the drug for which the subject is being treated.
    This is known specifically as

    A. substitution   B. cross-addiction
    C. surrender   D. submission

16. During an intervention, which of the following types of statements should be offered to the addicted person by members of the intervention team?

    A. Generalized comments
    B. Judgments
    C. Observations
    D. Opinions

17. Past failures, emotional trauma, and personality defects are examples of _____ factors in an individual's predisposition to addiction.

    A. genetic
    B. constitutional
    C. psychological
    D. sociocultural

18. The normalization process during the restabilization phase of recovery treatment includes

    A. introducing external motivations for recovery
    B. personality restructuring
    C. personality growth
    D. stress reduction techniques

19. Which characteristic typically differs between female and male alcoholics?

    A. Age
    B. Rate of advancement through addictive stages
    C. Likelihood of concurrent addiction to prescription drugs
    D. Professional status

20. Each of the following is an important factor determining the overall effects of addiction on a family EXCEPT

    A. the type of substance used
    B. the sex of addicted parent
    C. existing feelings of nonaddicted family members toward the addicted
    D. where and when substances are used

21. The component of a comprehensive addiction treatment program that is included in the category of psychosocial rehabilitation is

    A. social assessment
    B. treating medical problems
    C. random drug screenings
    D. detoxification

22. Each of the following is considered a warning sign for the onset of alcoholism's early stages EXCEPT

    A. alcohol-related problems
    B. hiding bottles
    C. changes in drinking patterns
    D. preoccupation with alcohol

23. If sedatives are to be used by a subject during the alcoholic withdrawal period, APPROXIMATELY how long is the recommended period for their use?

    A. For the first overnight period
    B. For the first three or four days
    C. Until the subject does not appear to require sedation
    D. Throughout the entire period of detoxification

24. Which of the following is NOT one of the psychological factors influencing addiction?

    A. Coping mechanisms   B. Denial
    C. Tolerance changes   D. Reinforcing factors

25. The characteristic of an addicted person's recovery illustrated by the person's acknowledgement of his/her individual responsibility for recovery is termed

    A. surrender   B. acceptance
    C. fellowship   D. admission

KEY (CORRECT ANSWERS)

1.	D	11.	D
2.	A	12.	C
3.	B	13.	D
4.	A	14.	D
5.	D	15.	B
6.	A	16.	C
7.	C	17.	C
8.	B	18.	D
9.	A	19.	C
10.	C	20.	A

21. C
22. B
23. B
24. C
25. B

EXAMINATION SECTION
TEST 1

DIRECTIONS: Each question or incomplete statement is followed by several suggested answers or completions. Select the one that BEST answers the question or completes the statement. *PRINT THE LETTER OF THE CORRECT ANSWER IN THE SPACE AT THE RIGHT.*

1. Which of the following symptoms, by itself, would NOT signify that a person receiving treatment for alcoholism might undergo a difficult period of withdrawal? 1.____

    A. Previous history of seizures or delirium tremens
    B. Ulcers or gastritis
    C. Irritability or depression
    D. Elevated blood pressure or pulse

2. In general, the format and direction of treatment for alcoholics and people dependent upon drugs should 2.____

    A. differ in intensity according to the progression of the addiction
    B. be flexible enough not to interfere with the patient's normal living patterns
    C. begin with immediate isolation
    D. remain the same for all patients

3. Which of the following words is NOT typically used to describe the disease of alcoholism? 3.____

    A. Chronic   B. Nonfatal
    C. Primary   D. Hereditary

4. Each of the following symptoms characterizes stage one in an alcoholic subject's withdrawal process EXCEPT 4.____

    A. auditory hallucinations   B. loss of appetite
    C. hand tremors   D. diarrhea

5. During the initial stages of recovery, which of the following vitamin supplements is NOT usually among the most important for the typically malnourished alcoholic subject? 5.____

    A. Zinc   B. Calcium
    C. B-complex   D. Vitamin C

6. What is the term for the point in recovery treatment that marks the clearest turning point, and signals that the subject has escaped immediate danger? 6.____

    A. Submission   B. Substitution
    C. Surrender   D. Synchronization

7. As a rule, _____ should always be excluded from the team making an intervention into an addicted person's life. 7.____

    A. staff members of a treatment facility
    B. people with abuse or addiction problems
    C. the addicted person's professional superiors
    D. members of the religious community

8. Approximately what percentage of untreated alcoholics will eventually experience delirium tremens?

   A. 10% B. 20% C. 30% D. 40%

9. Each of the following is considered to be one of the essential elements in subduing an addiction EXCEPT

   A. total abstinence
   B. firm but compassionate care
   C. nutritional repair
   D. vigorous physical exercise

10. Which of the following stages in the progression to freedom from addiction is considered to be the foundation on which all other elements are dependent?

    A. Spiritual well-being B. Mental well-being
    C. Total abstinence D. Physical well-being

11. Which of the following is a sign of early-stage addiction in an adolescent?

    A. Increase in tolerance B. Legal problems
    C. Changes in appearance D. Buying drugs

12. Which of the following is NOT normally included in the description of a *typical* alcoholic in the early stages of treatment?

    A. Withdrawn B. Suspicious
    C. Talks loudly D. Poorly groomed

13. Which of the following is considered to be an internal enabler for abuse or addiction?

    A. Modeling of use by parents
    B. Approval of use by peers
    C. The removal of deterrent consequences
    D. Rationalization of use

14. Approximately what percentage of alcoholics are heavy caffeine drinkers?

    A. 0-10% B. 10-15% C. 45-50% D. 90-95%

15. Good addiction treatment facilities have all of the following characteristics in common EXCEPT

    A. reliance on psychotherapy
    B. family involvement
    C. introduction and participation in AA or related groups
    D. occupational guidance

16. Which factor in an individual's predisposition to addiction is related to the biological differences between addicts and non-addicts?

    A. Genetic B. Constitutional
    C. Psychological D. Sociocultural

17. Typically, no detoxifying agents or drugs are used for the detoxification period during treatment for addiction to

   A. alcohol   B. opiates   C. cocaine   D. valium

18. Which of the following elements is considered to be unique to teenage alcoholism or addiction?

   A. Self-centeredness
   B. Peer pressure
   C. Rebelliousness
   D. Fear of life without drugs

19. A component of a comprehensive addiction treatment program that is included in the category of evaluation and assessment is

   A. treating physiological crises
   B. family therapy
   C. addiction screening
   D. stress reduction

20. The middle stages of alcoholism are often characterized by the onset of

   A. a progressive increase in drinking
   B. financial dependence
   C. guilty feelings
   D. alcohol-related arrests

21. Which of the following unconscious defense mechanisms, used by an addicted person, is characterized by blaming others for behaviors and consequences?

   A. Denial   B. Minimization
   C. Rationalization   D. Projection

22. Which of the following *leverages,* or inducements for voluntary submission to treatment, would be LEAST appropriate for use by members of an intervention team?

   A. Termination of employment
   B. Threat of divorce
   C. Threat of institutionalization
   D. Termination of friendship

23. Which of the following is NOT considered to be one of the primary goals in a structured detoxification process?

   A. Helping ease the pain associated with withdrawal
   B. Allowing the symptoms of withdrawal to run their natural course
   C. Correcting underlying medical problems or malnutrition
   D. Preparing patient for abstinence without dependence on other drugs

24. The _____ is ALWAYS a mistake on the part of treatment staff while the patient is going through the detoxification process.

   A. administration of narcotic sedatives
   B. prolonged isolation of the subject
   C. attempt to induce the subject's acknowledgment of his/her addiction
   D. liberal administration of multivitamin supplements

25. The enabling behaviors MOST likely to be practiced by the addicted person's family members in the intermediate stages of addiction are
    A. cooperation and collaboration
    B. protecting and shielding
    C. codependence and cohabitation
    D. control and guilt

25._____

KEY (CORRECT ANSWERS)

1. C
2. D
3. B
4. A
5. A

6. C
7. B
8. A
9. D
10. C

11. A
12. D
13. D
14. D
15. A

16. B
17. C
18. B
19. C
20. C

21. D
22. C
23. B
24. C
25. D

TEST 2

DIRECTIONS: Each question or incomplete statement is followed by several suggested answers or completions. Select the one that BEST answers the question or completes the statement. *PRINT THE LETTER OF THE CORRECT ANSWER IN THE SPACE AT THE RIGHT.*

1. Recurring withdrawal symptoms are LEAST common during the treatment for _____ addiction.

    A. alcohol B. valium C. amphetamine D. cocaine

    1.____

2. The normalization process during the posttreatment restructuring phase of recovery treatment includes

    A. increasing self-esteem through feedback
    B. learning communication skills
    C. a physical exercise program
    D. implementation of a healthy diet

    2.____

3. Stage three in an alcoholic's withdrawal process is characterized by

    A. delirium tremens B. seizures
    C. auditory hallucinations D. insomnia

    3.____

4. The characteristic of an addicted person's recovery illustrated by the person's acknowledgement of his/her addiction is termed

    A. surrender B. acceptance C. admission D. restitution

    4.____

5. During the early stages of recovery treatment, which of the following characteristics of a subject's expression or demeanor is usually NOT a cause for worry on the part of the treatment staff?

    A. Boredom B. Anxiety C. Aloofness D. Arrogance

    5.____

6. Which of the following steps should be taken FIRST by friends/family members who want to practice intervention in a person's addiction?

    A. Devising a treatment plan
    B. Confronting the addicted person
    C. Getting help for the person's family
    D. Asking others for help

    6.____

7. An addicted person who would require one of the less intense levels of recovery treatment and care would PROBABLY

    A. have chronic psychiatric problems
    B. lack family or social support
    C. already be resigned to treatment
    D. have family members who were also addicted

    7.____

8. The percentage of people with psychotic disorders among the alcoholic population is _____ that of the general population.

    A. half as much as B. no different than
    C. one a half times as much as D. twice as much as

    8.____

9. A recovering addict will typically experience the GREATEST risk of relapse during

   A. detoxification
   B. the first six months of treatment
   C. the second six months of treatment
   D. late stage recovery

10. The depressant which usually carries the GREATEST potential for dependency or abuse is

   A. valium   B. librium   C. halcion   D. seconal

11. Each of the following is considered to be a crucial element in the detoxification process EXCEPT

   A. stimulation   B. security   C. supplements   D. sedation

12. Which of the addiction risk factors is considered to be the MOST influential?

   A. Hereditary   B. Behavioral   C. Demographic   D. Psychiatric

13. The component of a, comprehensive addiction treatment program that is included in the category of medical and psychiatric management is

   A. detoxification
   B. recreation and leisure
   C. group therapy
   D. relapse prevention training

14. Which of the following is NOT typically a characteristic more pronounced in female alcoholics than in males?

   A. Greater degree of guilt
   B. More likely to feel locked into unhealthy relationships
   C. More likely to use illegal drugs
   D. More difficulty dealing with feelings of inadequacy

15. The information needed first to determine whether a person is addicted, and to which all other factors are secondary considerations, are the

   A. results of the person's physical examination
   B. person's performance level at home and on the job
   C. person's overall pattern of alcohol or drug use
   D. person's family medical history

16. Which of the following is considered part of the necessary treatment for an alcoholic subject who has entered stage one of the withdrawal process?

   A. Sedation
   B. Well-lit room
   C. Constant medical supervision
   D. Intravenous administration of fluid supplements

17. Mood-altering drugs are capable of each of the following EXCEPT

    A. causing psychiatric symptoms of varying intensity
    B. masking existing psychiatric symptoms and disorders
    C. curing certain psychiatric disorders
    D. initiate or worsen existing psychiatric disorders

18. When initially questioning a subject about his or her use of alcohol or drugs, the questioner should avoid asking, until the later stages of treatment, whether

    A. the subject drinks or uses drugs
    B. the subject has experienced any trouble related to the use of drugs or alcohol
    C. the subject feels any guilt about his/her use of drugs or alcohol
    D. any friends or relatives have had problems with drugs or alcohol

19. Elderly alcoholics typically differ from others in that they are MORE likely to

    A. deny their addiction
    B. combine their alcoholism with over-the-counter drug addiction
    C. begin their drinking in social settings
    D. become afflicted with alcoholism

20. The normalization process during the mature recovery phase of treatment includes

    A. personality restructuring
    B. introduction of normal sleep patterns
    C. personality growth
    D. stress reduction techniques

21. Which of the following is a sign that an adolescent has entered the intermediate stage of addiction?

    A. Denial
    B. Abuse as an act of defiance
    C. Increasing tolerance
    D. First blackouts

22. Which of the following is NOT one of the benefits associated with the use of sedatives during a subject's withdrawal period?

    A. Reduces fear of new surroundings and circumstances
    B. Shortens the time needed for detoxification
    C. Reduces likelihood of premature departure
    D. Prevents progression of withdrawal symptoms into advanced stages

23. Which stage in the progression to freedom from addiction is considered to be the intermediate level of recovery?

    A. Spiritual well-being   B. Mental well-being
    C. Total abstinence   D. Physical well-being

24. Each of the following symptoms typically signify that a drinker has progressed to the advanced stages of the alcoholic disease EXCEPT

    A. lack of attention to hygiene
    B. increased tolerance for alcohol
    C. morning drinking
    D. alcohol-related accidents

24.____

25. What is the typical percentage of alcoholic people entering treatment programs who will require the use of sedatives during withdrawal?

    A. 1-10%   B. 10-20%   C. 20-30%   D. 30-40%

25.____

KEY (CORRECT ANSWERS)

1. A		11. A	
2. A		12. A	
3. A		13. A	
4. C		14. C	
5. B		15. C	
6. D		16. B	
7. C		17. C	
8. B		18. C	
9. B		19. B	
10. D		20. A	

21. A
22. B
23. B
24. B
25. C

BASIC QUESTIONS AND ANSWERS ON ALCOHOL

TABLE OF CONTENTS

		Page
Introduction		1
I.	What is alcohol?	1
II.	How does alcohol work in the body?	1
III.	How fast does alcohol take effect?	2
IV.	Why do people drink?	2
V.	What is drunkenness?	3
VI.	What is a hangover?	3
VII.	What physical harm can heavy drinking cause?	3
VIII.	How can you tell if someone is alcoholic?	4
IX.	How can a person with an alcohol problem be helped?	4
X.	Can alcohol problems be prevented?	5

BASIC QUESTIONS AND ANSWERS ON ALCOHOL

HOW WIDELY ARE ALCOHOLIC BEVERAGES USED?

As far back as historical records go, beverages containing alcohol have been made and used by people. Such beverages are part of the cultures of peoples throughout the world.

In fact, two-thirds of the adult population in the United States do drink at least occasionally, while one-third do not drink at all. Among the youth of this country, a recent survey found that most American adolescents have had at least some experience with alcoholic beverages. Almost 80 percent have had at least one drink; about 74 percent have had at least two or three drinks; and over one-half of all adolescents drink at least once a month.

I. WHAT IS ALCOHOL?

Alcohol, the major active ingredient in wine, beer, and distilled liquor, is a natural substance formed by the reaction of fermenting sugar with yeast spores. There are many alcohols, but the kind in alcoholic beverages is ethyl alcohol -- a colorless, inflammable liquid with an intoxicating effect.

Ethyl alcohol is a drug which can produce feelings of well-being, sedation, intoxication, or unconsciousness--depending on the amount and the manner in which it is drunk. Technically, it can also be classified as a food, since it contains colories; however, it has no nutritional value.

Various alcoholic beverages are produced by using different sources of sugar for fermentation. For instance, beer is made from grapes or berries, whiskey from malted trains, and rum from molasses. Hard liquors--such as whiskey, gin, and vodka--are produced by distillation, which further concentrates the alcohol resulting from fermentation.

ALCOHOL CONTENT OF TYPICAL ALCOHOLIC BEVERAGES

Beer	- 4%
Dinner wine	- 10-12%
Fortified wine	- 17-20%
Distilled liquor	- 40-50%

Each fluid ounce of 100 percent alcohol contains about 200 calories, although the alcoholic beverages and drinks derived from them vary widely. About the same alcoholic content, one-half ounce of pure alcohol, is found in:

- a 12-ounce can of beer
- a 5-ounce glass of dinner wine
- a cocktail containing 1 1/2 ounces of 86-proof liquor

II. HOW DOES ALCOHOL WORK IN THE BODY?

Unlike other "food," alcohol does not have to be digested. When you drink an alcoholic beverage, 20 percent of the alcohol in it is absorbed immediately into the bloodstream through the stomach walls. The other 80 percent of the alcohol enters the bloodstream almost as fast after being quickly processed through the gastrointestinal tract. Moments after it is consumed, alcohol can be found in all tissues, organs, and secretions of the body. The alcohol eventually acts on the brain's central control areas to slow down or depress brain activity

A low level of alcohol in the blood, such as would result from sipping one drink--for example, a 12-ounce can of beer--has a mild tranquilzing effect on most people. Although basically a sedative, alcohol seems to act temporarily as a stimulant for many after they first start drinking. This is due to the fact that alcohol's initial effects are on those parts of the brain affecting learned behavior patterns such as self-control. After a drink or two, this learned behavior may temporarily disappear, making you lose your inhibitions, talk more freely, or feel like the "life of the party." On the other hand, you may feel aggressive or depressed.

Higher blood alcohol levels depress brain activity to the point that memory, as well as muscle coordination and balance, may be temporarily impaired. Still larger alcohol intake within a relatively short period of time depresses deeper parts of the brain, severely affecting judgment and dulling the senses.

If steady heavy drinking continues, the alcohol anesthetizes the deepest levels of the brain and can cause coma or death by depressing heart functions and breathing.

III. HOW FAST DOES ALCOHOL TAKE EFFECT?

The rapidity with which alcohol enters the bloodstream and exerts its effects on the brain and body depends on several factors:

How fast you drink. The half-ounce of pure alcohol in an average highball, can of beer, or glass of wine can be burned up or metabolized in the body in about 2 hours. If you sip your drink slowly and do not have more than one drink every 2 hours, the alcohol will not have a chance to jolt your brain or build up significantly in your blood, and you will feel little unpleasant effect. On the other hand, gulping drinks produces immediate, intoxicating effects and depression of deeper brain centers.

Whether your stomach is empty or full. Eating, especially before you drink but also while you drink, will slow down alcohol's rate of absorption into your bloodstream and produce a more even response to the alcohol.

What you drink. The alcohol in wine and beer is more diluted and is, therefore, absorbed somewhat more slowly into the bloodstream than alcohol from hard liquor. Diluting distilled spirits with water also helps to slow down absorption, but mixing with carbonated beverages can increase the rate of absorption.

How much you weigh. The effect of alcohol on the body varies according to a person's weight. Alcohol is quickly distributed uniformly within the circulatory system. Therefore, if the same amount is drunk by a 120-pound person and a 180-pound person, the alcohol is more concentrated in the bloodstream of the lighter individual and therefore more intoxicating to that person.

The setting, your mood or expectations. If you are sitting down relaxed while having a drink with a friend, alcohol will not affect you as much as when you are standing and drinking at a cocktail party. If you are emotionally upset, under stress, or tired, alcohol may have a stronger impact on you than normal. Your expectations will also have an influence. If you think you are going to become drunk, you are likely to get that way more quickly.

IV. WHY DO PEOPLE DRINK?

People drink for a variety of social, cultural, religious, or medical reasons. They drink at parties and celebrations with friends and relatives. They drink in religious ceremonies. Some drink wine to complement the taste of their dinners. Some drink to relax. Some drink to increase their appetites.

The drinking of most people is "integrative" drinking; that is, the use of alcohol is an adjunct to other activities, such as meals, family and religious feasts, or an evening with friends.

Among Orthodox Jews, native Italians, and other groups where alcohol is part of religious or social traditions, there is a low incidence of problem drinking, though there is almost universal use of alcoholic beverages.

There are, however, large numbers of people who drink for reasons that are not social, cultural, religious, or medical. They use alcohol to forget their worries, to escape from reality, or to gather courage to face the stresses of life. They are using alcohol as a drug and are in danger of becoming dependent upon it.

V. WHAT IS DRUNKENNESS?

Drunkenness is characterized by a temporary loss of control over physical and mental powers caused by excessive alcohol intake. Symp-toms of drunkenness vary, but they can include impaired vision, distorted depth perception, thick speech, and bad coordination. The ability to solve problems is reduced, emotion and mood become unpredictable, memory is impaired, and judgment becomes poor.

In most States a person is considered legally drunk when he or she has a 0.10 percent blood alcohol level. This means that one part in every thousand parts of the person's blood is presently composed of pure alcohol. Such a situation generally results when a person weighing about 160 pounds has had about seven drinks within 2 hours after eating. A person will reach this stage with fewer drinks if body weight is less than 160 pounds, with more drinks if weight exceeds this fugure. In a few States, the legally drunk level is 0.15 percent. In either case, it is illegal to drive a car after the specified blood alcohol concentration is reached.

Contrary to a widespread impression, one cannot sober up by such devices as drinking black coffee, taking a cold shower, or breathing pure oxygen. It takes a specific amount of time for the body to burn up a quantity of alcohol, generally at the rate of 7 grams (about 1/4 ounce) of pure alcohol per hour. The effect of drinking alcohol can be varied only by controlling the rate and concentration with which it is drunk. Once alcohol is in the bloodstream, nothing can be done about its effects except to wait until it is metabolized by the body.

VI. WHAT IS A HANGOVER?

A hangover is the body's reaction to excessive drinking. The associated miseries of nausea, gastritis, anxiety, and headache vary from case to case, but there is always extreme fatigue. No scientific evidence supports the curative claims for coffee, raw eggs, oysters, chili peppers, steak sauce, vitamins or other drugs, or the "hair of the dog." Doctors ususaly prescribe aspirin, rest, and solid food.

If you choose to drink, the best way to avoid a hangover is to avoid drunkenness. Sip slowly, with food in the stomach, under relaxed circumstances, and pay attention to your responses to the alcohol so you don't drink too much.

VII. WHAT PHYSICAL HARM CAN HEAVY DRINKING CAUSE?

Heavy drinking over time can cause severe physiological damage. Cirrhosis of the liver is closely linked to heavy, continuous consumption of alcohol, and there is also a link between this type of drinking and ulcers, heart disease, and diabetes. Heavy drinking over many years may also contribute to serious nervous or mental disorders, or may cause permanent brain damage. Alcohol, like many other drugs that affect the central nervous system, can be physiologically addictive, producing withdrawal symptoms when alcohol intake ceases.

Of course, drinking need not be long-term or addictive to cause accidental injury or death. Only two cans of beer or two drinks of 86-proof whiskey consumed by the average 160-pound person within an hour on an empty stomach generally result in a blood alcohol level of 0.05 percent—one part of alcohol in every 2,000 parts of blood. Scientific studies have revealed that even these small amounts limit coordination and increase a person's risk of becoming involved in a traffic or household accident. This often comes as a surprise to people being tested, since many feel more capable and mentally alert than they did before drinking.

VIII. HOW CAN YOU TELL IF SOMEONE IS ALCOHOLIC?

Alcoholism is marked by dependence on alcohol and loss of control over one's drinking. This loss of control may develop almost imperceptibly over a long period, or it may manifest itself almost from the start of a person's drinking. When a person continues to drink despite the fact that it causes serious psychological, physical, or social problems, alcoholism is developing or is already present.

We tend to think of "typical" alcohol people as skid row inhabitants, but only about 3-5 percent of alcoholic Americans are in that category. Actually, alcoholic people represent a cross-section of America, embracing rich and poor, young and old, white-collar workers and blue-collar workers--in fact, every level of society. Most alcoholics are employed and most have families--much like their neighbors and fellow citizens.

Seldom can you spot alcoholic people by their appearance. However, for those close to a person who seems to be more and more dependent on alcohol in order to function, there are indicators that his or her drinking may be reaching the danger point. For example is there the immediate reaction to pour a drink when faced with any problem; has getting drunk become a regular occurrence; is there a record of missing work because of drinking or regular attendance at work with an ill-disguised odor of liquor on the breath; has the person's license been suspended for driving while drunk; has the person gotten into trouble with authorities for no "logical" reason; has the person been involved in several unexplainable accidents without evidence of physical impairment; has his or her home life become intolerable because of excessive drinking or arguments resulting from drinking?

When such signs are present, it means that a person's drinking pattern, if not already out of control, is heading that way.

IX. HOW CAN A PERSON WITH AN ALCOHOL PROBLEM BE HELPED?

In the past, most people believed that nothing could be done for a person with a drinking problem. It is now recognized that the overwhelming number can be helped at any stage so long as adequate treatment and rehabilitation resources are available, care is marked by acceptance and understanding, and the stigma of having an alcohol problem is not allowed to stand in the way of treatment.

Help can be provided by a doctor, a clergyman, a local welfare agency, a clinic, a social worker, a psychologist or psychiatrist, a general hospital or psychiatric hospital, an alcoholism treatment cen-ter, or the local chapter of Alcoholics Anonymous. Many large business or industrial firms and labor unions also have programs to help their alcoholic employees and members find treatment and rehabilitation.

Alcoholics Anonymous is probably the best known source of help for alcoholic persons. This organization is a self-help group in which members help each other in a type of group therapy setting that utilizes mutual experience for mutual support. Alcoholics Anonymous is listed in all local directories.

Other community and social agencies also offer referral services or direct help. Local affiliates of the National Council on Alcoholism exist in many communities, and every State and many communities have official alcoholism programs where help can be found or sources of treatment recommended. Again, the local telephone directory is the key to obtaining their services.

The treatment used for alcoholism is as varied as the reasons for alcoholic drinking, and programs which individualize the treatment approaches to the patient's needs offer the best results. Doctors may prescribe a drug, Antabuse, which makes an alcoholic person violently ill if he or she drinks alcohol. Psychotherapy and counseling may be used to provide long-range help. Although considerable success has been reported in nonmedical, social setting withdrawal from alcohol, in the case of acute alcoholism or acute intoxication, hospitalization may be required for a short period of time.

The primary goal of treatment is to help the person overcome his dependence on alcohol and develop a lifestyle not revolving around its use. Experience to date has been that the chances of improvement seem greatest if total abstinence is the goal. As many as two-thirds of the people who seek help recover from alcoholism, a figure that compares favorably with the results of treatment for other psychological or behavioral problems.

It is almost universally recognized today that alcoholism affects others besides the alcoholic individual--especially those close to the drinker. To meet this need, Al-Anon Family Groups were set up to assist the families--principally spouses--and more recently Alateen came into existence to help the adolescent children of alcoholic persons.

X. CAN ALCOHOL PROBLEMS BE PREVENTED?

Problem drinking and alcoholism can never be controlled solely by treating people. The long-range goal must be prevention; and this requires education, both in the schools and in the adult community, to develop the Nation's habits of mederation in the use of alcoholic beverages and to encourage respect for those who choose to abstain. It also requires investigation and testing of such social policies as control of distribution and availability, excise taxes, etc., as well as study of the effective prevention policies of other cultures.

One immediate step that we as individuals can take toward preventing alcohol problems in our own social circles is assuming the responsibilities that we as hosts and hostesses have to our friends. At dinner parties and social gatherings, food should be served both before and with drinks. As an alternative to alcoholic beverages, soft drinks--including low-calorie beverages--should be made available. These can be supplemented by nonalcoholic punches, fruit juices, tea,and coffee. The guest who does not choose to drink alcoholic beverages should never be cajoled or shamed into doing so, whether he is an abstainer, a recovered alcoholic, or a social drinker who recognizes he has had enough. One effective method of giving your guests some extra time for alcohol effects to wear off is to close the bar at least 1 or 2 hours before you plan to break up your party. This is the time to drink coffee and other nonalcoholic beverages and to serve your own special highlight dish of meat or seafood.

DRUG ABUSE

CONTENTS

The Controlled Substances Act
I Controlling Drugs or Other Substances ... 1
    Formal Scheduling ... 1
    Schedule I ... 3
    Schedule II ... 3
    Schedule III ... 3
    Schedule IV ... 3
    Schedule V. ... 4
    Emergency or temporary Scheduling. ... 4
    Controlled Substance Analogues. ... 5
    International Treaty Obligation. ... 5

II Regulation ... 5
    Registration ... 5
    Recordkeeping ... 5
    Distribution ... 6
    Dispensing to Patients ... 6
    Quotas ... 7
    Security ... 7

III Penalties ... 7
    User Accountability/ Personal Use Penalties ... 7
    User Accountability ... 8
    Personal Use Amounts ... 8

Narcotics
Narcotics of Natural Origin ... 11
    Opium ... 11
    Morphine ... 12
    Codeine ... 12
    Thebaine ... 12

Semi-Synthetic Narcotics ... 12
    Heroin ... 12
    Hydromorphone ... 13
    Oxycodone ... 13
    Hydrocodone ... 13

Synthetic Narcotics ... 13
    Meperidine ... 13
    Methadone and Related Drugs ... 13
    Fentanyl ... 14
    Pentazocine ... 14

Depressants
    Chloral Hydrate ... 16
    Barbiturates ... 16
    Glutethimide and Methqualone ... 16
    Meporobamate ... 17
    Benzodiazepines ... 17

Stimulants
    Cocaine ... 18
    Amphetamines ... 19
    Methcathinone ... 20
    Khat ... 20
    Methylphenidate (Ritalin) ... 20
    Anorectic Drugs ... 21

Hallucinogens
Naturally Occurring Hallucinogens ... 22
    Peyote and Mescaline ... 22
    Psilocybin and Psilocyn ... 23
    Dimethyltryptamine (DMT) ... 23
    LSD ... 23
    DOM, DOB, MDA, AND MDM and 2C-B ... 24
    Phencyclidine (PCP) And Related drugs ... 24

Cannabis
Marijuana ... 25
Hash ... 26
Hashis Oil ... 26

Steroids
Anabolic Steroids ... 27

Related Topics
Clandestine ... 28
Inhalants ... 28

Controlled Substances Uses & Effects (Chart) ... 30
    Schedule II ... 31
    Schedule IV ... 31

DRUG ABUSE
CONTROLLED SUBSTANCES ACT

The Controlled Substances Act (CSA), Title II of the Comprehensive Drug Abuse Prevention and Control Act of 1970, is the legal foundation of the government's fight against abuse of drugs and other substances. This law is a consolidation of numerous laws regulating the manufacture and distribution of narcotics, stimulants, depressants, hallucinogens, anabolic steroids and chemicals used in the illicit production of controlled substances.

CONTROLLING DRUGS OR OTHER SUBSTANCES

FORMAL SCHEDULING

The CSA places all substances which were in some manner regulated under existing Federal law into one of five schedules. This placement is based upon the substance's medical use, potential for abuse, and safety or dependence liability. The Act also provides a mechanism for substances to be controlled, or added to a schedule; decontrolled, or removed from control; and rescheduled or transferred from one schedule to another. The procedure for these actions is found in Section 201 of the Act (21 D.S.C. 811).

Proceedings to add, delete, or change the schedule of a drug or other substance may be initiated by the Drug Enforcement Administration (DEA), the Department of Health and Human Services (HHS), or by petition from any interested party: the manufacturer of a drug, a medical society or association, a pharmacy association, a public interest group concerned with drug abuse, a state or local government agency, or an individual citizen. When a petition is received by DEA, the agency begins its own investigation of the drug.

The agency also may begin an investigation of a drug at any time based upon information received from law enforcement laboratories, state and local law enforcement and regulatory agencies, or other sources of information.

Once DEA has collected the necessary data, the Administrator of DEA, by authority of the Attorney General, requests from HHS a scientific and medical evaluation and recommendation as to whether the drug or other substance should be controlled or removed from control. This request is sent to the Assistant Secretary of Health of HHS. HHS solicits information from the Commissioner of the Food and Drug Administration (FDA), evaluations and recommendations from the National Institute on Drug Abuse, and on occasion from the scientific and medical community at large. The Assistant Secretary, by authority of the Secretary, compiles the information and transmits back to DEA a medical and scientific evaluation regarding the drug or other substance, a recommendation as to whether the drug should be controlled, and in what schedule it should be placed.

The medical and scientific evaluations are binding on DEA with respect to scientific and medical matters. The recommendation on scheduling is binding only to the extent that if HHS recommends that the substance not be controlled, DEA may not control the substance.

Once DEA has received the scientific and medical evaluation from HHS, the Administrator will evaluate all available data and make a final decision whether to propose that a drug or other substance should be controlled and into which schedule it should be placed.

The threshold issue is whether the drug or other substance has potential for abuse. If a drug does not have a potential for abuse, it cannot be controlled. Although the term "potential for abuse" is not defined in the CSA, there is much discussion of the term in the legislative history of the Act. The following items are indicators that a drug or other substance has a potential for abuse:

1) There is evidence that individuals are taking the drug or other substance in amounts sufficient to create a hazard to their health or to the safety of other individuals or to the community; or

2) There is significant diversion of the drug or other substance from legitimate drug channels; or

3) Individuals are taking the drug or other substance on their own initiative rather than on the basis of medical advice from a practitioner licensed by law to administer such drugs; or

4) The drug is a new drug so related in its action to a drug or other substance already listed as having a potential for abuse to make it likely that the drug will have the same potential for abuse as such drugs, thus making it reasonable to assume that there may be significant diversions from legitimate channels, significant use contrary to or without medical advice, or that it has a substantial capability of creating hazards to the health of the user or to the safety of the community. Of course, evidence of actual abuse of a substance is indicative that a drug has a potential for abuse.

In determining into which schedule a drug or other substance should be placed, or whether a substance should be decontrolled or rescheduled, certain factors are required to be considered. Specific findings are not required for each factor. These factors are listed in Section 201 (c), [21 U.S.C. 811 (c)], of the CSA and are as follows:

1) *The drug's actual or relative potential for abuse.*

2) *Scientific evidence of the drug's pharmacological effects.* The state of know 1edge with respect to the effects of a specific drug is, of course, a major consideration. For example, it is vital to know whether or not a drug has a hallucinogenic effect if it is to be controlled because of that. The best available knowledge of the pharmacological properties of a drug should be considered.

3) *The state of current scientific knowledge regarding the substance.* Criteria (2) and (3) are closely related. However, (2) is primarily concerned with pharmacological effects and (3) deals with all scientific knowledge with respect to the substance.

4) *Its history and current pattern of abuse.* To determine whether or not a drug should be controlled, it is important to know the pattern of abuse of that substance, including the socio-economic characteristics of the segments of the population involved in such abuse.

5) *The scope, duration, and significance of abuse.* In evaluating existing abuse, the Administrator must know not only the pattern of abuse but whether the abuse is widespread. In reaching his decision, the Administrator should consider the economics of regulation and enforcement attendant to such a decision. In addition, he should be aware of the social significance and impact of such a decision upon those people, especially the young that would be affected by it.

6) *What, if any, risk there is to the public health.* If a drug creates dangers to the public health, in addition to or because of its abuse potential, then these dangers must also be considered by the Administrator.

7) *The drug's psychic or physiological dependence liability.* There must be an assessment of the extent to which a drug is physically addictive or psychologically habit-forming, if such information is known.

8) *Whether the substance is an immediate precursor of a substance already controlled.* The CSA allows inclusion of immediate precursors on this basis alone into the appropriate schedule and thus safeguards against possibilities of clandestine manufacture.

After considering the above listed factors, the Administrator must make specific findings concerning the drug or other substance. This will determine into which schedule the drug or other substance will be placed. These schedules are established by the CSA. They are as follows:

Schedule I

- The drug or other substance has a high potential for abuse.
- The drug or other substance has no currently accepted medical use in treatment in the United States.
- There is a lack of accepted safety for use of the drug or other substance under medical supervision.
- Some Schedule I substances are heroin, LSD, marijuana, and methamphetamine

Schedule II

- The drug or other substance has a high potential for abuse.
- The drug or other substance has a currently accepted medical use in treatment in the United States or a currently accepted medical use with severe restrictions.
- Abuse of the drug or other substance may lead to severe psychological or physical dependence.
- Schedule II substances include morphine, PCP, cocaine, methadone, and methamphetamine.

Schedule III

- The drug or other substance has a potential for abuse less than the drugs or other substances in Schedules I and II.
- The drug or other substance has a currently accepted medical use in treatment in the United States.
- Abuse of the drug or other substance may lead to moderate or low physical dependence or high psychological dependence.
- Anabolic steroids, codeine and hydrocodone with aspirin or Tylenol®, and some barbiturates are Schedule III substances.

Schedule IV

- The drug or other substance has a low potential for abuse relative to the drugs or other substances in Schedule III.
- The drug or other substance has a currently accepted medical use in treatment in the United States.
- Abuse of the drug or other substance may lead to limited physical dependence or psychological dependence relative to the drugs or other substances in Schedule III.
- Included in Schedule IV are Darvon®, Talwin®, Equanil®, Valium® and Xanax®.

Schedule V

- The drug or other substance has a low potential for abuse relative to the drugs or other substances in Schedule IV.
- The drug or other substance has a currently accepted medical use in treatment in the United States.
- Abuse of the drug or other substances may lead to limited physical dependence or psychological dependence relative to the drugs or other substances in Schedule IV.
- Over-the-counter cough medicines with codeine are classified in Schedule V.

When the Administrator of DEA has determined that a drug or other substance should be controlled, decontrolled, or rescheduled, a proposal to take action is published in the F federal Register. The proposal invites all interested persons to file comments with DEA. Affected parties may also request a hearing with DEA. If no hearing is requested, DEA will evaluate all comments received and publish a final order in the Federal Register, controlling the drug as proposed or with modifications based upon the written comments filed. This order will set the effective dates for imposing the various requirements imposed under the CSA.

If a hearing is requested, DEA will enter into discussions with the party or parties requesting a hearing in an attempt to narrow the issue for litigation. If necessary, a hearing will then be held before an Administrative Law Judge. The judge will take evidence on factual issues and hear arguments on legal questions regarding the control of the drug. Depending on the scope and complexity of the issues, the hearing may be brief or quite extensive. The Administrative Law Judge, at the close of the hearing, prepares findings of fact and conclusions of law and a recommended decision which is submitted to the Administrator of DEA. The Administrator will review these documents, as well as the underlying material, and prepare his/her own findings of fact and conclusions of law (which may or may not be the same as those drafted by the Administrative Law Judge). The Administrator then publishes a final order in the Federal Register either scheduling the drug or other substance or declining to do so.

Once the final order is published in the *Federal Register*, interested parties have 30 days to appeal to a U.S. Court of Appeals to challenge the order. Findings of fact by the Administrator are deemed conclusive if supported by "substantial evidence." The order imposing controls is not stayed during the appeal, however, unless so ordered by the Court.

Emergency or Temporary Scheduling

The CSA was amended by the Comprehensive Crime Control Act of 1984. This Act included a provision which allows the Administrator of DE A to place a substance, on a temporary basis, into Schedule I when necessary to avoid an imminent hazard to the public safety.

This emergency scheduling authority permits the scheduling of a substance which is not currently controlled, is being abused, and is a risk to the public health while the formal rule making procedures described in the CSA are being conducted. This emergency scheduling applies only to substances with no accepted medical use. A temporary scheduling order may be issued for one year with a possible extension of up to six months if formal scheduling procedures have been initiated. The proposal and order are published in the Federal Register as are the proposals and orders for formal scheduling. [21 V.S.C. 811 (1)]

Controlled Substance Analogues

A new class of substances was created by the Anti-Drug Abuse Act of 1986. Controlled substance analogues are substances which are not controlled substances, but may be found in the illicit traffic. They are structurally or pharmacologically similar to Schedule I or II controlled substances and have no legitimate medical use. A substance which meets the definition of a controlled substance analogue and is intended for human consumption is treated under the CSA as if it were a controlled substance in Schedule I.

International Treaty Obligations

U. S. treaty obligations may require that a drug or other substance be controlled under the CSA, or rescheduled if existing controls are less stringent than those required by a treaty. The procedures for these scheduling actions are found in Section 201 (d) of the Act. [21 V.S.C. 811 (d)]

The United States is a party to the Single Convention on Narcotic Drugs of 1961, designed to establish effective control over international and domestic traffic in narcotics, coca leaf, cocaine, and cannabis. A second treaty, the Convention on Psychotropic Sub- stances of 1971, which entered into force in 1976, is designed to establish comparable control over stimulants, depressants, and hallucinogens. Congress ratified this treaty in 1980.

II. REGULATION

The CSA creates a closed system of distribution for those authorized to handle controlled substances. The cornerstone of this system is the registration of all those authorized by DEA to handle controlled substances. All individuals and firms that are registered are required to maintain complete and accurate inventories and records of all transactions involving controlled substances, as well as security for the storage of controlled substances.

Registration

Any person who handles or intends to handle controlled substances must obtain a registration issued by DEA. A unique number is assigned to each legitimate handler of controlled drugs: importer, exporter, manufacturer, distributor, hospital, pharmacy, practitioner, and researcher. This number must be made available to the supplier by the customer prior to the purchase of a controlled substance. Thus, the opportunity for unauthorized transactions is greatly diminished.

Recordkeeping

The CSA requires that complete and accurate records be kept of all quantities of controlled substances manufactured, purchased, and sold. Each substance must be inventoried every two years. Some limited exceptions to the recordkeeping requirements may apply to certain categories of registrants.

From these records it is possible to trace the flow of any drug from the time it is first imported or manufactured through the distribution level, to the pharmacy or hospital that dispensed it, and then to the actual patient who received the drug. The mere existence of this requirement is sufficient to discourage many forms of diversion. It actually serves large drug corporations as an internal check to uncover diversion, such as pilferage by employees.

There is one distinction between scheduled items for recordkeeping requirements. Records for Schedule I and II drugs must be kept separate from all other records of the handler; records for Schedule III, IV, and V substances must be kept in a "readily retrievable" form. The former method allows for more expeditious investigations involving the highly abusable substances in Schedules I and II.

Distribution

The keeping of records is required for distribution of a controlled substance from one manufacturer to another, from manufacturer to distributor, and from distributor to dispenser. In the case of Schedule I and II drugs, the supplier must have a special order form from the customer. This order form (DEA Form 222) is issued by DEA only to persons who are properly registered to handle Schedules I and II. The form is preprinted with the name and address of the customer. The drugs must be shipped to this name and address. The use of this device is a special reinforcement of the registration requirement; it makes doubly certain that only authorized individuals may obtain Schedule I and II drugs. Another benefit of the form is the special monitoring it permits. The form is issued in triplicate: the customer keeps one copy; two copies go to the supplier who, after filling the order, keeps a copy and forwards the third copy to the nearest DEA office.

For drugs in Schedules III, IV, and V, no order form is necessary. The supplier in each case, however, is under an obligation to verify the authenticity of the customer. The supplier is held fully accountable for any drugs which are shipped to a purchaser who does not have a valid registration.

Manufacturers must submit periodic reports of the Schedule I and II controlled substances they produce in bulk and dosage forms. They also report the manufactured quantity and form of each narcotic substance listed in Schedules III, IV, and V, as well as the quantity of synthesized psychotropic substances listed in Schedules I, II, III, and IV. Distributors of controlled substances must report the quantity and form of all their transactions of controlled drugs listed in Schedules I and II and narcotics listed in Schedule III. Both manufacturers and distributors are required to provide reports of their annual inventories of these controlled substances. This data is entered into a system called the Automated Reports and Consolidated Orders System (ARCOS). It enables DEA to monitor the distribution of controlled substances throughout the country, and to identify retail level registrants that receive unusual quantities of controlled substances.

Dispensing to Patients

The dispensing of a controlled substance is the delivery of the controlled substance to the ultimate user, who may be a patient or research subject. Special control mechanisms operate here as well. Schedule I drugs are those which have no currently accepted medical use in the United States; they may, therefore, be used in the United States only in research situations. They generally are supplied by only a limited number of firms to properly registered and qualified researchers. Controlled substances may be dispensed by a practitioner by direct administration, by prescription, or by dispensing from office supplies. Records must be maintained by the practitioner of all dispensing of controlled substances from office supplies and of certain administrations. The CSA does not require the practitioner to maintain copies of prescriptions, but certain states require the use of multiple copy prescriptions for Schedule II and other specified controlled substances.

The determination to place drugs on prescription is within the jurisdiction of the FDA. Unlike other prescription drugs, however, controlled substances are subject to additional restrictions. Schedule II prescription orders must be written and signed by the practitioner; they may not be telephoned into the pharmacy except in an emergency. In addition, a prescription for a Schedule II drug may not be refilled; the patient must see the practitioner again in order to obtain more drugs. For Schedule III and IV drugs, the prescription order may be either written or oral (that is, by telephone to the pharmacy). In addition, the patient may (if authorized by the practitioner) have the prescription refilled up to five times and at any time within six months from the date of the initial dispensing.

Schedule V includes some prescription drugs and many over-the-counter narcotic preparations, including antitussives and antidiarrheal. Even here, however, the law imposes restrictions beyond those normally required for the over-the-counter sales; for example, the patient must be at least 18 years of age, must offer some form of identification, and have his or her name entered into a special log maintained by the pharmacist as part of a special record.

Quotas

DEA limits the quantity of Schedule I and II controlled substances which may be produced in the United States in any given calendar year. By utilizing available data on sales and inventories of these controlled substances, and taking into account estimates of drug usage provided by the FDA, DEA establishes annual aggregate production quotas for Schedule I and II controlled substances. The aggregate production quota is allocated among the various manufacturers who are registered to manufacture the specific drug. DEA also allocates the amount of bulk drug which may be procured by those companies which prepare the drug into dosage units.

Security

DEA registrants are required by regulation to maintain certain security for the storage and distribution of controlled substances. Manufacturers and distributors of Schedule I and II substances must store controlled substances in specially constructed vaults or highly rated safes, and maintain electronic security for all storage areas. Lesser physical security requirements apply to retail level registrants such as hospitals and pharmacies.

All registrants are required to make every effort to ensure that controlled substances in their possession are not diverted into the illicit market. This requires operational as well as physical security. For example, registrants are responsible for ensuring that controlled substances are distributed only to other registrants that are authorized to receive them or to legitimate patients and consumers.

III. PENALTIES

The CSA provides penalties for unlawful manufacturing, distribution, and dispensing of controlled substances. The penalties are basically determined by the schedule of the drug or other substance, and sometimes are specified by drug name, as in the case of marijuana. As the statute has been amended since its initial passage in 1970, the penalties have been altered by Congress. The charts on pages 8 and 9 are an overview of the penalties for trafficking or unlawful distribution of controlled substances. This is not inclusive of the penalties provided under the CSA.

User Accountability/Personal Use Penalties

On November 19, 1988, Congress passed the Anti-Drug Abuse Act of 1988, P. L. 100690. Two sections of this Act represent the Federal Government's attempt to reduce drug abuse by dealing not just with the person who sells the illegal drug, but also with the person who buys it. The first new section is titled "User Accountability" and is codified at 21 U.S.C. § 862 and various sections of Title 42, U.S.C. The second involves "personal use amounts" of illegal drugs, and is codified at 21 U.S.C. § 844a.

User Accountability

The purpose of User Accountability is to not only make the public aware of the Federal Government's position on drug abuse, but to describe new programs intended to decrease drug abuse by holding drug abusers personally responsible for their illegal activities, and imposing civil penalties on those who violate drug laws.

It is important to remember that these penalties are in addition to the criminal penalties drug abusers are already given, and do not replace those criminal penalties.

The new User Accountability programs call for more instruction in schools, kindergarten through senior high, to educate children on the dangers of drug abuse. These programs will include participation by students, parents, teachers, local businesses and the local, state and Federal Government.

User Accountability also targets businesses interested in doing business with the Federal Government. This program requires those businesses to maintain a drug free workplace, principally through educating employees on the dangers of drug abuse, and by informing employees of the penalties they face if they engage in illegal drug activity on company property.

There is also a provision in the law that makes public housing projects drug-free by evicting those residents who allow their units to be used for illegal drug activity, and denies Federal benefits, such as housing assistance and student loans, to individuals convicted of illegal drug activity. Depending on the offense, an individual may be prohibited from ever receiving any benefit provided by the Federal Government.

Personal Use Amounts

This section of the 1988 Act allows the government to punish minor drug offenders without giving the offender a criminal record if the offender is in possession of only a small amount of drugs. This law is designed to impact the "user" of illicit drugs, while simultaneously saving the government the costs of a full-blown criminal investigation.

Under this section, the government has the option of imposing only a civil fine on individuals possessing only a small quantity of an illegal drug. Possession of this small quantity, identified as a "personal use amount" carries a civil fine of up to $10,000.

In determining the amount of the fine in a particular case, the drug offender's income and assets will be considered. This is accomplished through an administrative proceeding rather than a criminal trial, thus reducing the exposure of the offender to the entire criminal justice system, and reducing the costs to the offender and the government.

The value of this section is that it allows the government to punish a minor drug offender without saddling the offender with a criminal record. This section also gives the drug offender the opportunity to fully redeem himself or herself, and have all public record of the proceeding destroyed. If this was the drug offender's first offense, and the offender has paid all fines, can pass a drug test, and has not been convicted of a crime after three years, the offender can request that all proceedings be dismissed.

If the proceeding is dismissed, the drug offender can lawfully say he or she had never been prosecuted, either criminally or civilly, for a drug offense.

Congress has imposed two limitations on this section's use. It may not be used if (1) the drug offender has been previously convicted of a Federal or state drug offense; or (2) the offender has already been fined twice under this section.

NARCOTICS

The term narcotic, derived from the Greek word for stupor, originally referred to a variety of substances that induced sleep. In a legal context, narcotic refers to opium, opium derivatives and their semisynthetic or totally synthetic substitutes. Cocaine and coca leaves, which are classified as "narcotics" in the Controlled Substances Act (CSA), are technically not narcotics and are discussed in the section on stimulants.

Narcotics can be administered in a variety of ways. Some are taken orally, transdermally (skin patches) or injected. They are also available in suppositories. As drugs of abuse, they are often smoked, sniffed or self-administered by the more direct routes of subcutaneous ("skin popping") and intravenous ("mainlining") injection.

Drug effects depend heavily on the dose, route of administration, previous exposure to the drug and the expectation of the user. Aside from their clinical use in the treatment of pain, cough suppression and acute diarrhea, narcotics produce a general sense of well-being by reducing tension, anxiety, and aggression. These effects are helpful in a therapeutic setting but contribute to their abuse.

Narcotic use is associated with a variety of unwanted effects including drowsiness, inability to concentrate, apathy, lessened physical activity, constriction of the pupils, dilation of the subcutaneous blood vessels causing flushing of the face and neck, constipation, nausea and vomiting and, most significantly, respiratory depression. As the dose is increased, the subjective, analgesic, and toxic effects become more pronounced. Except in cases of acute intoxication, there is no loss of motor coordination or slurred speech as occurs with many depressants.

Among the hazards of illicit drug use is the ever increasing risk of infection, disease and overdose. Medical complications common among narcotic abusers arise primarily from adulterants found in street drugs and in the non-sterile practices of injecting. Skin, lung and brain abscesses, endocarditis, hepatitis and AIDS are commonly found among narcotic abusers. Since there is no simple way to determine the purity of a drug that is sold on the street, the effects of illicit narcotic use are unpredictable and can be fatal.

With repeated use of narcotics, tolerance and dependence develop. The development of tolerance is characterized by a shortened duration and a decreased intensity of analgesia, euphoria and sedation which creates the need to administer progressively larger doses to attain the desired effect. Tolerance does not develop uniformly for all actions of these drugs, giving rise to a number of toxic effects. Although the lethal dose is increased significantly in tolerant users, there is always a dose at which death can occur from respiratory depression.

Physical dependence refers to an alteration of nor" mal body functions that necessitates the continued presence of a drug in order to prevent the withdrawal or abstinence syndrome. The intensity and character of the physical symptoms experienced during withdrawal are directly related to the particular drug of abuse, the total daily dose, the interval between doses, the duration of use and the health and personality of the addict. In general, narcotics with shorter durations of action tend to produce shorter, more intense withdrawal symptoms, while drugs that produce longer narcotic effects have prolonged symptoms that tend to be less severe.

The withdrawal symptoms experienced from heroin/morphine-like addiction are usually experienced shortly before the time of the next scheduled dose. Early symptoms include watery eyes, runny nose, yawning and sweating. Restlessness, irritability, loss of appetite, tremors and severe sneezing appear as the syndrome progresses. Severe depression and vomiting are not uncommon. The heart rate and blood pressure are elevated. Chills alternating with flushing and excessive sweating are also characteristic symptoms. Pains in the bones and muscles of the back and extremities occur as do muscle spasms and kicking movements, which may be the source of the expression "kicking the habit." At any point during this process, a suitable narcotic can be administered that will dramatically reverse the withdrawal symptoms. Without intervention, the syndrome will run its course and most of the overt physical symptoms will disappear within 7 to 10 days.

The psychological dependence that is associated with narcotic addiction is complex and protracted. Long after the physical need for the drug has passed, the addict may continue to think and talk about the use of drugs. There is a high probability that relapse will occur after narcotic withdrawal when neither the physical environment nor the behavioral motivators that contributed to the abuse have been altered.

There are two major patterns of narcotic abuse or dependence seen in the U.S. One involves individuals whose drug use was initiated within the context of medical treatment who escalate their dose through "doctor shopping" or branch out to illicit drugs. A very small percentage of addicts are in this group

The other more common pattern of abuse is initiated outside the therapeutic setting with experimental or recreational use of narcotics. The majority of individuals in this category may abuse narcotics sporadically for months or even years. These occasional users are called "chippers." Although they are neither tolerant of nor dependent on narcotics, the social, medical and legal consequences of their behavior is very serious. Some experimental users will escalate their narcotic use and will eventually become dependent, both physically and psychologically. The earlier drug use begins, the more likely it is to progress to abuse and dependence. Heroin use among males in inner cities is generally initiated in adolescence and dependence develops in about 1or 2 years.

Narcotics of Natural Origin

The poppy *Papaver somniferum* is the source for non-synthetic narcotics. It was grown in the Mediterranean region as early as 5000 B.C., and has since been cultivated in a number of countries throughout the world. The milky fluid that seeps from incisions in the unripe seedpod of this poppy has, since ancient times, been scraped by hand and air dried to produce what is known as opium. A more modern method of harvesting is by the industrial poppy straw process of extracting alkaloids from the mature dried plant. The extract may be in liquid, solid or powder form, although most poppy straw concentrate available commercially is a fine brownish powder. More than 500 tons of opium or their equivalents in poppy straw concentrate are legally imported into the U.S. annually for legitimate medical use.

Opium - There were no legal restrictions on the importation or use of opium until the early 1900s. In the United States, the unrestricted availability of opium, the influx of opium smoking immigrants from the Orient, and the invention of the hypodermic needle contributed to the more severe variety of compulsive drug abuse seen at the turn of this century. In those days, medicines often contained opium without any warning label. Today there are state, federal and international laws governing the production and distribution of narcotic substances.

Although opium is used in the form of paragoric to treat diarrhea, most opium imported into the United States is broken down into its alkaloid constituents. These alkaloids are divided into two distinct chemical classes, phenanthrenes and isoquinolines. The principal phenanthrenes are morphine, codeine and thebaine, while the isoquinolines have no significant central nervous system effects and are not regulated under the CSA.

Morphine - Morphine, the principal constituent of opium, can range in concentration from 4 to 21 percent (note: commercial opium is standardized to contain 10% morphine). It is one of the most effective drugs known for the relief of pain, and remains the standard against which new analgesics are measured. Morphine is marketed in a variety of forms including oral solutions (Roxanol), sustained release tablets (MSIR and MS-Contin), suppositories and injectable preparations. It may be administered orally, subcutaneously, intramuscularly, or intravenously, the latter method being the one most frequently used by addicts. Tolerance and physical dependence develop rapidly in the user. Only a small part of the morphine obtained from opium is used directly; most of it is converted to codeine and other derivatives.

Codeine - This alkaloid is found in opium in concentrations ranging from 0.7 to 2.5 percent. Most codeine used in the U.S. is produced from morphine. Compared to morphine, codeine produces less analgesia, sedation and respiratory depression and is frequently taken orally. Codeine is medically prescribed for the relief of moderate pain. It is made into tablets either alone or in combination with aspirin or acetaminophen (Tylenol). Codeine is an effective cough suppressant and is found in a number of liquid preparations. Codeine products are also used to a lesser extent, as an injectable solution for the treatment of pain. It is by far the most widely used naturally occurring narcotic in medical treatment in the world. Codeine products are encountered on the illicit market frequently in combination with glutethimide (Doriden) or carisoprodol (Soma).

Thebaine - A minor constituent of opium, thebaine is chemically similar to both morphine and codeine, but produces stimulatory rather than depressant effects. Thebaine is not used therapeutically, but is converted into a variety of compounds including codeine, hydrocodone, oxycodone, oxymorphone, nalbuphine, naloxone, naltrexone and buprenorphine. It is controlled in Schedule II of the CSA as well as under international law.

Semi-Synthetic Narcotics

The following narcotics are among the more significant substances that have been derived by modification of the phenanthrene alkaloids contained in opium:

Heroin - First synthesized from morphine in 1874, heroin was not extensively used in medicine until the beginning of this century. Commercial production of the new pain remedy was first started in 1898. While it received widespread acceptance from the medical profession, physicians remained unaware of its potential for addiction for years. The first comprehensive control of heroin in the United States was established with the Harrison Narcotic Act of 1914.

Pure heroin is a white powder with a bitter taste. Most illicit heroin is a powder which may vary in color from white to dark brown because of impurities left from the manufacturing process or the presence of additives. Pure heroin is rarely sold on the street. A "bag"-slang for a single dosage unit of heroin-may contain 100 mg of powder, only a portion of which is heroin; the remainder could be sugars, starch, powdered milk, or quinine. Traditionally the purity of heroin in a bag has ranged from 1 to 10 percent; more recently heroin purity has ranged from 1 to 98 percent, with a national average of 35 percent.

Another form of heroin known as "black tar" has also become increasingly available in the western United States. The color and consistency of black tar heroin result from the crude processing methods used to illicitly manufacture heroin in Mexico. Black tar heroin may be sticky like roofing tar or hard like coal, and its color may vary from dark brown to black. Black tar heroin is often sold on the street in its tar-like state at purities ranging from 20 to 80 percent. Black tar heroin is most frequently dissolved, diluted and injected.

The typical heroin user today consumes more heroin than a typical user did just a decade ago, which is not surprising given the higher purity currently available at the street level. Until recently, heroin in the United States almost exclusively was injected either intravenously, subcutaneously (skin-popping), or intramuscularly. Injection is the most practical and efficient way to administer low-purity heroin. The availability of higher purity heroin has meant that users now can snort or smoke the narcotic. Evidence suggests that heroin snorting is widespread or increasing in those areas of the country where high-purity heroin is available, generally in the northeastern United States. This method of administration may be more appealing to new users because it eliminates both the fear of acquiring syringe-borne diseases such as HIV / AIDS and hepatitis, and the historical stigma attached to intravenous heroin use.

Hydromorphone - Hydromorphone (Dilaudid) is marketed both in tablet and injectable forms. Its analgesic potency is from two to eight times that of morphine. Much sought after by narcotic addicts, hydromorphone is usually obtained by the abuser through fraudulent prescriptions or theft. The tablets are dissolved and injected as a substitute for heroin

Oxycodone - Oxycodone is synthesized from thebaine. It is similar to codeine, but is more potent and has a higher dependence potential. It is effective orally and is marketed in combination with aspirin (Percodan) or acetaminophen (Percocet) for the relief of pain. Addicts take these tablets orally or dissolve them in water, filter out the insoluble material, and "mainline" the active drug.

Hydrocodone - Hydrocodone is an orally active analgesic and antitussive Schedule II narcotic which is marketed in multi-ingredient Schedule III products. The therapeutic dose of 5-10 mg is pharmacologically equivalent to 60 mg of oral morphine. Sales and production of this drug have increased significantly in recent years as have diversion and illicit use. Trade names include Anexsia, Hycodan, Hycomine, Lorcet, Lortab, Tussionex, Tylox and Vicodin. These are available as tablets, capsules and/or syrups.

Synthetic Narcotics

In contrast to the pharmaceutical products derived directly or indirectly from narcotics of natural origin, synthetic narcotics are produced entirely within the laboratory. The continuing search for products that retain the analgesic properties of morphine without the consequent dangers of tolerance and dependence has yet to yield a product that is not susceptible to abuse. A number of clandestinely-produced drugs as well as drugs that have accepted medical uses fall into this category.

Meperidine - Introduced as a potent analgesic in the 1930s, meperidine produces effects that are similar but not identical to morphine (shorter duration of action and reduced antitussive and antidiarrheal actions). Currently it is used for the relief of moderate to severe pain, particularly in obstetrics and post-operative situations. Meperdine is available in tablets, syrups and injectable forms (Demerol). Several analogues of meperidine have been clandestinely produced. One noteworthy analogue is a preparation with a neurotoxic by-product that has produced irreversible Parkinsonism.

Methadone and Related Drugs - German scientist's synthesized methadone during World War II because of a shortage of morphine. Although chemically unlike morphine or heroin, methadone produces many of the same effects. Introduced into the United States in 1947 as an analgesic (Dolophine), it is primarily used today for the treatment of narcotic addiction (Methadone). The effects of methadone are longer-lasting than those of morphine based drugs. Methadone's effects can last up to 24 hours, thereby permitting administration only once a day in heroin detoxification and maintenance programs. Methadone is almost as effective when administered orally as it is by injection. Tolerance and dependence may develop, and withdrawal symptoms, though they develop more slowly and are less severe than those of morphine and more slowly and are less severe than those of morphine and heroin, are more prolonged. Ironically, methadone used to control narcotic addiction is frequently encountered on the illicit market and has been associated with a number of overdose deaths.

Closely related to methadone, the synthetic compound levo-alphacetylmethadol or LAAM (ORLAAM) has an even longer duration of action (from 48 to 72 hours), permitting a reduction in frequency of use. In 1994 it was approved as a treatment of narcotic addiction. Buprenorphine (Buprenex), a semi-synthetic Schedule V narcotic analgesic derived from thebaine, is currently being investigated as a treatment of narcotic addiction.

Another close relative of methadone is dextropropoxyphene, first marketed in 1957 under the trade name of Darvon. Oral analgesic potency is one-half to one-third that of codeine, with 65 mg approximately equivalent to about 600 mg of aspirin. Dextroproxyphene is prescribed for relief of mild to moderate pain. Bulk dextropropoxyphene is in Schedule II, while preparations containing it are in Schedule IV. More than 100 tons of dextropropoxyphene are produced in the U.S. annually, and more than 25 million prescriptions are written for the products. This narcotic is associated with a number of toxic side effects and is among the top 10 drugs reported by medical examiners in drug abuse deaths.

Fentanyl - First synthesized in Belgium in the late 1950s, fentanyl was introduced into clinical practice in the 1960s as an intravenous anesthetic under the trade name of Sublimaze. Thereafter, two other fentanyl analogues were introduced: alfentanil (Alfenta), an ultra-short (5-10 minutes) acting analgesic, and sufentanil (Sufenta), an exceptionally potent analgesic for use in heart surgery. Today fentanyls are extensively used for anesthesia and analgesia. Illicit use of pharmaceutical fentanyls first appeared in the mid-1970s in the medical community and continues to be a problem in the U.S. To date, over 12 different analogues of fentanyl have been produced clandestinely and identified in the U.S. drug traffic. The biological effects of the fentanyls are indistinguishable from those of heroin with the exception that the fentanyls may be hundreds of times more potent. Fentanyls are most commonly used by intravenous administration, but like heroin, they may be smoked or snorted.

Pentazocine - The effort to find an effective analgesic that is less dependence-producing led to the development of pentazocine (Talwin). Introduced as an analgesic in 1967, it was frequently encountered in the illicit trade, usually in combination with tripelennamine and placed into Schedule IV in 1979. An attempt at reducing the abuse of this drug was made with the introduction of Talwin Nx. This product contains a quantity of antagonist sufficient to counteract the morphine-like effects of pentazocine if the tablets are dissolved and injected.

DEPRESSANTS

Historically, people of almost every culture have used chemical agents to induce sleep, relieve stress, and allay anxiety. While alcohol is one of the oldest and most universal agents used for these purposes, hundreds of substances have been developed that produce central nervous system (CNS) depression. These drugs have been referred to as "downers," sedatives, hypnotics, minor tranquilizers, anxiolytics, and antianxiety medications. Unlike most other classes of drugs of abuse, depressants, except for methaqualone, are rarely produced in clandestine laboratories. Generally, legitimate pharmaceutical products are diverted to the illicit market.

Although a number of depressants (i.e., chloral hydrate, glutethimide, meprobamate and methaqualone) have been important players in the milieu of depressant use and abuse, two major groups of depressants have dominated the licit and illicit market for nearly a century, first barbiturates and now benzodiazepines.

Barbiturates were very popular in the first half of this century. In moderate amounts, these drugs produce a state of intoxication that is remarkably similar to alcohol intoxication. Symptoms include slurred speech, loss of motor coordination and impaired judgment. Depending on the dose, frequency, and duration of use, one can rapidly develop tolerance, physical dependence and psychological dependence on barbiturates. With the development of tolerance, the margin of safety between the effective dose and the lethal dose becomes very narrow. That is, in order to obtain the same level of intoxication, the tolerant abuser may raise his or her dose to a level that can produce coma and death. Although many individuals have taken barbiturates therapeutically without harm, concern about the addiction potential of barbiturates and the ever-increasing numbers of fatalities associated with them led to the development of alternative medications. Today, only about 20% of all depressant prescriptions in the U.S. are for barbiturates.

Benzodiazepines were first marketed in the 1960s. Touted as much safer depressants with far less addiction potential than barbiturates, these drugs today account for about 30% of all prescriptions for controlled substances. It has only been recently that an awareness has developed that benzodiazepines share many of the undesirable side effects of the barbiturates. A number of toxic CNS effects are seen with chronic high dose benzodiazepine therapy. These include headache, irritability, confusion, memory impairment, depression, insomnia and tremor. The risk of developing over-sedation, dizziness and confusion increases substantially with higher doses of benzodiazepines. Prolonged use can lead to physical dependence even at recommended dosages. Unlike barbiturates, large doses of benzodiazepines are rarely fatal unless combined with other drugs or alcohol. Although primary abuse of benzodiazepines is well documented, abuse of these drugs usually occurs as part of a pattern of multiple drug abuse. For example, heroin or cocaine abusers will use benzodiazepines and other depressants to augment their "high" or alter the side effects associated with over-stimulation or narcotic withdrawal.

There are marked similarities among the withdrawal symptoms seen with all drugs classified as depressants. In its mildest form, the withdrawal syndrome may produce insomnia and anxiety, usually the same symptoms that initiated the drug use. With a greater level of dependence, tremors and weakness are also present, and in its most severe form, the withdrawal syndrome can cause seizures and delirium. Unlike the withdrawal syndrome seen with most other drugs of abuse, withdrawal from depressants can be life-threatening

Chloral Hydrate

The oldest of the hypnotic (sleep inducing) depressants, chloral hydrate was first synthesized in 1832. Marketed as syrups or soft gelatin capsules, chloral hydrate takes effect in a relatively short time (30 minutes) and will induce sleep in about an hour. A solution of chloral hydrate and alcohol
constituted the infamous "knockout drops" or "Mickey Finn." At therapeutic doses, chloral hydrate has little effect on respiration and blood pressure but, a toxic dose produces severe respiratory depression and very low blood pressure. Although chloral hydrate is still encountered today, its use declined with the introduction of the barbiturates

Barbiturates

Barbiturates (derivatives of barbituric acid) were first introduced for medical use in the early 1900s. More than 2,500 barbiturates have been synthesized, and in the height of their popularity about 50 were marketed for human use. Today, only about a dozen are used. Barbiturates produce a wide spectrum of CNS depression, from mild sedation to coma, and have been used as sedatives, hypnotics, anesthetics and anticonvulsants.

The primary differences among many of these products are how fast they produce an effect and how long those effects last. Barbiturates are classified as ultrashort, short, intermediate and long-acting.

The ultrashort-acting barbiturates produce anesthesia within about one minute after intravenous administration. Those in current medical use are methohexital (Brevital), thiamylal (Surital) and thiopental (Pentothal).

Barbiturate abusers prefer the short-acting and intermediate-acting barbiturates pentobarbital (Nembutal), secobarbital (Seconal) and amobarbital (Amytal). Other short- and intermediate-acting barbiturates are butalbital (Fiorinal, Fioricet), butabarbital (Butisol), talbutal (Lotusate) and aprobarbital (Alurate). After oral administration, the onset of action is from 15 to 40 minutes and the effects last up to 6 hours. These drugs are primarily used for sedation or to induce sleep. Veterinarians use pentobarbital for anesthesia and euthanasia.

Long-acting barbiturates include phenobarbital (Luminal) and mephobarbital (Mebaral). Effects of these drugs are realized in about one hour and last for about 12 hours and are used primarily for daytime sedation and the treatment of seizure disorders or mild anxiety.

Glutethimide and Methqualone

Glutethimide (Doriden) was introduced in 1954 and methaqualone (Quaalude, Sopor) in 1965 as safe barbiturate substitutes. Experience showed, however, that their addiction liability and the severity of withdrawal symptoms were similar to those of barbiturates. By 1972, "luding out," taking methaqualone with wine, was a popular college pastime. Excessive use leads to tolerance, dependence and withdrawal symptoms similar to those of barbiturates. Overdose by glutethimide and methaqualone is more difficult to treat than barbiturate overdose, and deaths have frequently occurred. In the United States, the marketing of methaqualone pharmaceutical products stopped in 1984 and methaqualone was transferred to Schedule I of the CSA. In 1991, glutethimide was transferred into Schedule II in response to an upsurge in the prevalence of diversion, abuse and overdose deaths.

Meprobamate

Meprobamate was introduced as an antianxiety agent in 1955 and is prescribed primarily to treat anxiety, tension and associated muscle spasms. More than 50 tons are distributed annually in the U.S. under its generic name and brand names such as Miltown and Equanil. Its onset and duration of action are similar to the intermediate acting barbiturates; however, therapeutic doses of meprobamate produce less sedation and toxicity than barbiturates. Excessive use can result in psychological and physical dependence.

Benzodiazepines

The benzodiazepine family of depressants is used therapeutically to produce sedation, induce sleep, relieve anxiety and muscle spasms and to prevent seizures. In general, benzodiazepines act as hypnotics in high doses, as anxiolytics in moderate doses and as sedatives in low doses. Of the drugs marketed in the United States that affect CNS function, benzodiazepines are among the widely prescribed medications and, unfortunately, are frequently abused. Fifteen members of this group are presently marketed in the United States and an additional twenty are marketed in other countries.

Like the barbiturates, benzodiazepines differ from one another in how fast they take effect and how long the effects last. Shorter acting benzodiazepines, used to manage insomnia, include estazolam (ProSom), flurazepam (Dalmane), quazepam (Doral), temazepam (Restoril) and triazolam (Halcion).

Benzodiazepines with longer durations of action include alprazolam (Xanax), chlordiazepoxide (Librium), clorazepate (Tranxene), diazepam (Valium), halazepam (Paxipam), lorazepam (Ativan), oxazepam (Serax) and prazepam (Centrax). These longer acting drugs are primarily used for the treatment of general anxiety. Midazolam (Versed) is available in the U.S. only in an injectable form for an adjunct to anesthesia. Clonazepam (Klonopin) is recommended for use in the treatment of seizure disorders.

Flunitrazepam (Rohypnol), which produces diazepam-like effects, is becoming increasingly popular among young people as a drug of abuse. The drug is not marketed legally in the United States, but is smuggled in by traffickers.

Benzodiazepines are classified in the CSA as Schedule IV depressants. Repeated use of large doses or, in some cases, daily use of therapeutic doses of benzodiazepines is associated with physical dependence. The withdrawal syndrome is similar to that of alcohol withdrawal and is generally more unpleasant and longer lasting than narcotic withdrawal and frequently requires hospitalization. Abrupt cessation of benzodiazepines is not recommended and tapering-down the dose eliminates many of the unpleasant symptoms.

Given the number of people who are prescribed benzodiazepines, relatively few patients increase their dosage or engage in drugseeking behavior. However, those individuals who do abuse benzodiazepines often maintain their drug supply by getting prescriptions from several doctors, forging prescriptions or buying diverted pharmaceutical products on the illicit market. Abuse is frequently associated with adolescents and young adults who take benzodiazepines to obtain a "high." This intoxicated state results in reduced inhibition and impaired judgment. Concurrent use of a1cohol or other depressants with benzodiazepines can be life-threatening. Abuse of benzodiazepines is particularly high among heroin and cocaine abusers. Approximately 50 percent of people entering treatment for narcotic or cocaine addiction also report abusing benzodiazepines.

STIMULANTS

Stimulants are sometimes referred to as "uppers" and reverse the effects of fatigue on both mental and physical tasks. Two commonly used stimulants are nicotine, found in tobacco products, and caffeine, an active ingredient in coffee, tea, some soft drinks and many non-prescription medicines. Used in moderation, these substances tend to relieve malaise and increase alertness. Although the use of these products has been an accepted part of our culture, the recognition of their adverse effects has resulted in a proliferation of caffeine-free products and efforts to discourage cigarette smoking.

A number of stimulants, however, are under the regulatory control of the CSA. Some of these controlled substances are available by prescription for legitimate medical use in the treatment of obesity, narcolepsy and attention deficit hyperactivity disorders. As drugs of abuse, stimulants are frequently taken to produce a sense of exhilaration, enhance self-esteem, improve mental and physical performance, increase activity, reduce appetite, produce prolonged wakefulness, and to "get high." They are recognized as among the most potent agents of reward and reinforcement that underlie the problem of dependence.

Stimulants are both diverted from legitimate channels and clandestinely manufactured exclusively for the illicit market. They are taken orally, sniffed, smoked and injected. Smoking, snorting or injecting stimulants produces a sudden sensation known as a "rush" or a "flash." Abuse is often associated with a pattern of binge use that is, consuming large doses of stimulants sporadically. Heavy users may inject themselves every few hours, continuing until they have depleted their drug supply or reached a point of delirium, psychosis and physical exhaustion. During this period of heavy use, all other interests become secondary to recreating the initial euphoric rush. Tolerance can develop rapidly, and both physical and psychological dependence occur. Abrupt cessation, even after a weekend binge, is commonly followed by depression, anxiety, drug craving and extreme fatigue ("crash").

Therapeutic levels of stimulants can produce exhilaration, extended wakefulness and loss of appetite. These effects are greatly intensified when large doses of stimulants are taken. Physical side effects-including dizziness, tremor, headache, flushed skin, chest pain with palpitations, excessive sweating, vomiting and abdominal cramps-may occur as a result of taking too large a dose at one time or taking large doses over an extended period of time. Psychological effects include agitation, hostility, panic, aggression and suicidal or homicidal tendencies. Paranoia, sometimes accompanied by both auditory and visual hallucinations, may also occur. In overdose, unless there is medical intervention, high fever, convulsions and car- diovascular collapse may precede death. Because accidental death is partially due to the effects of stimulants on the body's cardiovascular and temperature-regulating systems, physical exertion increases the hazards of stimulant use.

Cocaine

Cocaine, the most potent stimulant of natural origin, is extracted from the leaves of the coca plant (Erythroxylon coca) which is indigenous to the Andean highlands of South America. Natives in this region chew or brew coca leaves into a tea for refreshment and to relieve fatigue similar to the customs of chewing tobacco and drinking tea or coffee.

Pure cocaine was first isolated in the 1880s and used as a local anesthetic in eye surgery. It was particularly useful in surgery of the nose and throat because of its ability to provide anesth-

anesthesia as well as to constrict blood vessels and limit bleeding. Many of its therapeutic applications are now obsolete due to the development of safer drugs.

Illicit cocaine is usually distributed as a white crystalline powder or as an off-white chunky material. The powder, usually cocaine hydrochloride, is often diluted with a variety of substances, the most common of which are sugars such as lactose, inositol and mannitol, and local anesthetics such as lidocaine. The adulteration increases the volume and thus multiplies profits. Cocaine hydrochloride is generally snorted or dissolved in water and injected. It is rarely smoked.

"Crack," the chunk or "rock" form of cocaine, is a ready-to-use freebase. On the illicit market it is sold in small, inexpensive dosage units that are smoked. With crack came a dramatic increase in drug abuse problems and violence. Smoking delivers large quantities of cocaine to the lungs producing effects comparable to intravenous injection; these effects are felt almost immediately after smoking, are very intense, and are quickly over. Once introduced in the mid-1980s, crack abuse spread rapidly and made the cocaine experience available to anyone with $10 and access to a dealer. In addition to other toxicities associated with cocaine abuse, cocaine smokers suffer from acute respiratory problems including cough, shortness of breath, and severe chest painswitll lung trauma and bleeding.

The intensity of the psychological effects of cocaine, as with most psychoactive drugs, depends on the dose and rate of entry to the brain. Cocaine reaches the brain through the snorting method in three to five minutes. Intravenous injection of cocaine produces a rush in 15 to 30 seconds and smoking produces an almost immediate intense experience. The euphoric effects of cocaine are almost indistinguishable from those of amphetamine, although they do not last as long. These intense effects can be followed by a dysphoric crash. To avoid the fatigue and the depression of "coming down," frequent repeated doses are taken. Excessive doses of cocaine may lead to seizures and death from respiratory failure, stroke, cerebral hemorrhage or heart failure. There is no specific antidote for cocaine overdose.

According to the 1993 Household Drug Survey, the number of Americans who used cocaine within the preceding month of the survey numbered about 1.3 million; occasional users (those who used cocaine less often than monthly) numbered at approximately 3 million, down from 8.1 million in 1985. The number of weekly users has remained steady at around a half million since 1983.

Amphetamines

Amphetamine, dextroamphetamine and methamphetamine are collectively referred to as amphetamines. Their chemical properties and actions are so similar that even experienced users have difficulty knowing which drug they have taken.

Amphetamine was first marketed in the 1930s as Benzedrine in an over-the-counter inhaler to treat nasal congestion. By 1937 amphetamine was available by prescription in tablet form and was used in the treatment of the sleeping disorder narcolepsy and the behavioral syndrome called minimal brain dysfunction (MBD), which today is called attention deficit hyperactivity disorder (ADHD). During World War II, amphetamine was widely used to keep the fighting men going; both dextroamphetamine (Dexedrine) and methamphetamine (Methedrine) became readily available. As use of amphetamines spread, so did their abuse. Amphetamines became a cureall for helping truckers to complete their long routes without falling asleep, for weight control, for helping athletes to perform better and train longer, and for treating mild depression. Intravenous amphetamine abuse spread among a subculture known as "speed freaks." With experience, it became evident that the dangers of abuse of these drugs outweighed most of their therapeutic uses.

Increased control measures were initiated in 1965 with amendments to the federal food and drug laws to curb the black market in amphetamines. Many pharmaceutical amphetamine products were removed from the market and doctors prescribed those that remained less freely. In order to
meet the everincreasing black market demand for amphetamines, clandestine laboratory's. production mushroomed, especially methamphetamine laboratories on the West Coast. Today, most amphetamines distributed to the black market are produced in clandestine laboratories.

Amphetamines are generally taken orally or injected. However, the addition of "ice," the slang name for crystallized methamphetamine hydrochloride, has promoted smoking as another mode of administration. Just as "crack" is smokable cocaine, "ice" is smokable methamphetamine. Both drugs are highly addictive and toxic.

The effects of amphetamines, especially methamphetamine, are similar to cocaine, but their onset is slower and their duration is longer. In general, chronic abuse produces a psychosis that resembles schizophrenia and is characterized by paranoia, picking at the skin, preoccupation with one's own thoughts, and auditory and visual hallucinations. Violent and erratic behavior is frequently seen among chronic abusers of amphetamines.

Methcathinone

Methcathinone is one of the more recent drugs of abuse in the U.S. and was placed into Schedule I of the CSA in 1993. Known on the streets as "Cat," it is a structural analogue of methamphetamine and cathinone. Clandestinely manufactured, methcathinone is almost exclusively sold in the stable and highly water soluble hydrochloride salt form. It is most commonly snorted, although it can be taken orally by mixing it with a beverage or diluted in water and injected intravenously. Methcathinone has an abuse potential equivalent to methamphetamine, and produces amphetamine-like activity including superabundant energy, hyperactivity, extended wakefulness and loss of appetite. Pleasant effects include a burst of energy, speeding of the mind, increased feelings of invincibility and euphoria. Unpleasant effects include anxiety, tremor, insomnia, weight loss, dehydration, sweating, stomach pains, pounding heart, nose bleeds and body aches. Toxic levels may produce convulsions, paranoia, and hallucinations. Like other CNS stimulants, binges are usually followed by a "crash" with periods of variable depression.

Khat

For centuries, khat, the fresh young leaves of the Catha edulis shrub, has been consumed where the plant is cultivated, primarily in East Africa and the Arabian Peninsula. There, chewing khat predates the use of coffee and is used in a similar social context. Chewed in moderation, khat alleviates fatigue and reduces appetite. Compulsive use may result in manic behavior with grandiose delusions or in a paranoid type of illness, some- times accompanied by hallucinations.

Khat has been brought into the U.S. and other countries for use by emigrants from the source countries. It contains a number of chemicals among which are two controlled substances, cathinone (Schedule I) and cathine (Schedule IV). As the leaves mature or dry, cathinone is converted to cathine which significantly reduces its stimulatory properties.

Methylphenidate (Ritalin)

The primary, legitimate medical use of methylphenidate (Ritalin) is to treat attention deficit disorders in children. As with other Schedule II stimulants, the abuse of methylphenidate may produce the same effects as the abuse of cocaine or the amphetamines. It has been reported that the psychosis of chronic methylphenidate intoxication is identical to the paranoid psychosis of amphetamine intoxication. Unlike other stimulants, however, methylphenidate has not been clandestinely produced, although abuse of this substance has been well documented among narcotic addicts who dissolve the tablets in water and inject the mixture. Complications arising from this practice are common due to the insoluble fillers used in the tablets. When injected, these materials block small blood vessels, causing serious damage to the lung and retina of the eye.

Anorectic Drugs

A number of drugs have been developed and marketed to replace amphetamines as appetite suppressants. These anorectic drugs include benzphetamine (Didrex), diethylproprion (Tenuate, Tepanil), fenfluramine (Pondimin), mazindol (Sanorex, Mazanor), phendimetrazine (Bontril, Prelu-l, Plegine) and phentermine (Ionamin, AdipexP). They produce many of the effects of the amphetamines, but are generally less potent. All are controlled under the CSA because of the similarity of their effects to those of the amphetamines.

HALLUCINOGENS

Hallucinogens are amoung the oldest known group of drugs that have been used for their ability to alter human perception and mood. For centuries, many of the naturally occurring hallucinogens found in plants and fungi have been used for medical, social, and religious practices. In more recent years, a number of synthetic hallucinogens have been produced, some of which are much more potent than their naturally occurring counterparts.

The biochemical, pharmacological and physiological basis for hallucinogenic activity is not well understood. Even the name for this class of drugs is not ideal, since hallucinogens do not always produce hallucinations. However, taken in nontoxic dosages, these substances produce changes in perception, thought and mood. Physiological effects include elevated heart rate, increased blood pressure and dilated pupils. Sensory effects include perceptual distortions that vary with dose, setting and mood. Psychic effects include disorders of thought associated with time and space. Time may appear to stand still and forms and colors seem to change and take on new significance. This experience may be pleasurable or extremely frightening. It needs to be stressed that the effects of hallucinogens are unpredictable each time they are used.

Weeks or even months after some hallucinogens have been taken; the user may experience flashbacks-fragmentary recurrences of certain aspects of the drug experience in the absence of actually taking the drug. The occurrence of a flashback is unpredictable, but is more likely to occur during times of stress and seem to occur more frequently in younger individuals. With time, these episodes diminish and become less intense.

The abuse of hallucinogens in the United States reached a peak in the late 1960s. A subsequent decline in their use may be attributed to real or perceived hazards associated with taking these drugs. However, a resurgence of use of hallucinogens in the 1990s, especially at the junior high school level, is cause for concern.

There is a considerable body of literature that links the use of some of the hallucinogenic substances to neuronal damage in animals; however, there is no conclusive scientific data that links brain or chromosomal damage to the use of hallucinogens in humans. The most common danger of hallucinogen use is impaired judgment that often leads to rash decisions and accidents.

NATURALLY OCCURRING HALLUCINOGENS

Peyote and Mescaline

Peyote is a small, spineless cactus, Lophophora williamsii, whose principal active ingredient is the hallucinogen mescaline. From earliest recorded time, peyote has been used by natives in northern Mexico and southwestern United States as a part of traditional religious rites. The top of the cactus above ground-also referred to as the crown-consists of disc-shaped buttons that are cut from the roots and dried. These buttons are generally chewed or soaked in water to produce an intoxicating liquid. The hallucinogenic dose for mescaline is about 0.3 to 0.5 grams (equivalent to about 5 grams of dried peyote) and lasts about 12 hours. While peyote produced rich visual hallucinations which were important to the native peyote cults, the full spectrum of effects served as a chemically induced model of mental illness. Mescaline can be extracted from peyote or produced synthetically.

Psilocybin and Psilocyn

Psilocybin and psilocyn are both chemicals obtained from certain mushrooms found in Mexico and Central America. Like peyote, the mushrooms have been used in native rites for centuries. Dried mushrooms contain about 0.2 to 0.4 percent psilocybin and only trace amounts of psilocyn. The hallucinogenic dose of both substances is about 4 to 8 milligrams or about 2 grams of mushrooms with effects lasting for about six hours. Both psilocybin and psilocyn can be produced synthetically.

Dimethyltryptamine (DMT)

Dimethyltryptamine, (DMT) has a long history of use worldwide as it is found in a variety of plants and seeds and can also be produced synthetically. It is ineffective when taken orally unless combined with another drug that inhibits its metabolism. Generally it is sniffed, smoked or injected. The effective hallucinogenic dose in humans is about 50 to 100 milligrams and lasts for about 45 to 60 minutes. Because the effects last only about an hour, the experience was called a "businessman's trip."

A number of other hallucinogens have very similar structures and properties to those of DMT. Diethyltryptamine (DET), for example, is an analogue of DMT and produces the same pharmacological effects but is somewhat less potent than DMT. Alphaethyltryptamine (AET) is another tryptamine hallucinogen recently added to the list of Schedule I substances in the CSA.

LSD

Lysergic acid diethylamide (LSD) is the most potent and highly studied hallucinogen known to man. It was originally synthesized in 1938 by Dr. Albert Hoffman, but its hallucinogenic effects were unknown until 1943 when Hoffman accidently consumed some LSD. It was later found that an oral dose of as little as 0.025 mg (or 25 micrograms, equal to a few grains of salt) was capable of producing rich and vivid hallucinations.

Because of its structural similarity to a chemical present in the brain and its similarity in effects to certain aspects of psychosis, LSD was used as a research tool to study mental illness. Although there was a decline in its illicit use from its initial popularity in the 1960s, LSD is making a comeback in the 1990s. The average effective oral dose is from 20 to 80 micrograms with the effects of higher doses lasting for 10 to 12 hours. LSD is usually sold in the form of impregnated paper (blotter acid), tablets (microdots), or thin squares of gelatin (window panes).

Physical reactions may include dilated pupils, lowered body temperature, nausea, "goose bumps," profuse perspiration, increased blood sugar and rapid heart rate. During the first hour after ingestion, the user may experience visual changes with extreme changes in mood. In the hallucinatory state, the user may suffer impaired depth and time perception accompanied by distorted perception of the size and shape of objects, movements, color, sound, touch and the user's own body image. During this period, the user's ability to perceive objects through the senses is distorted. He may describe "hearing colors" and "seeing sounds." The ability to make sensible judgments and see common dangers is impaired, making the user susceptible to personal injury. He may also injure others by attempting to drive a car or by operating machinery. After an LSD "trip," the user may suffer acute anxiety or depression for a variable period of time. Flashbacks have been reported days or even months after taking the last dose.

DOM, DOB, MDA, MDMA and 2C-B

Many chemical variations of mescaline and amphetamine have been synthesized for their "feel good" effects. 4-Methyl-2, 5dimethoxyamphetamine (DaM) was introduced into the San Francisco drug scene in the late 1960s, and was nicknamed STP, an acronym for "Serenity, Tranquillity, and Peace." Doses of 1 to 3 milligrams generally produce mood alterations and minor perceptual alterations while larger doses can produce pronounced hallucinations that last from 8 to 10 hours.

Other illicitly manufactured analogues include 4-bromo- 2,5-dimethoxyamphetamine (DaB), 3,4-methylenedioxyamphetamine (MD A), 3,4- methy lenedioxymethamphetamine (MDMA, also referred to as Ecstasy or XTC) and 4-bromo-2,5-dimethoxyphenethylamine (2C-B, NEXUS). These drugs differ from one another in their potency, speed of onset, duration of action and their capacity to modify mood with or without producing overt hallucinations. These drugs are widely used at "raves." (Raves are large all-night dance parties held in unusual settings, such as warehouses or railroad yards, that feature computer-generated, high volume, pulsating music.) The drugs are usually taken orally, sometimes snorted and rarely injected. Because they are produced in clandestine laboratories, they are seldom pure and the amount in a capsule or tablet is likely to vary considerably.

Phencyclidine (PCP) and Related Drugs

In the 1950s, phencyclidine was investigated as an anesthetic but, due to the side effects of confusion and delirium, its development for human use was discontinued. It became commercially available for use as a veterinary anesthetic in the 1960s under the trade name of Semylan and was placed in Schedule III of the CSA. In 1978, due to considerable abuse of phencyclidine, it was transferred to Schedule II of the CSA and manufacturing of Semylan was discontinued. Today, virtually all of the phencyclidine encountered on the illicit market in the U.S. is produced in clandestine laboratories. Phencyclidine, more commonly known as PCP, is illicitly marketed under a number of other names including Angel Dust, Supergrass, Killer Weed, Embalming Fluid, and Rocket Fuel, reflecting the range of its bizarre and volatile effects. In its pure form, it is a white crystalline powder that readily dissolves in water. However, most PCP on the illicit market contains a number of contaminates as a result of makeshift manufacturing causing the color to range from tan to brown and the consistency from powder to a gummy mass. Although sold in tablets and capsules as well as in powder and liquid form, it is commonly applied to a leafy material, such as parsley, mint, oregano or marijuana, and smoked.

The drug's effects are as varied as its appearance. A moderate amount of PCP often causes the user to feel detached, distant and estranged from his surroundings. Numbness, slurred speech and loss of coordination may be accompanied by a sense of strength and invulnerability. A blank stare, rapid and involuntary eye movements, and an exaggerated gait are among the more observable effects. Auditory hallucinations, image distortion, severe mood disorders, and amnesia may also occur. In some users, PCP may cause acute anxiety and a feeling of impending doom, in others paranoia and violent hostility, and in some it may produce a psychoses indistinguishable from schizophrenia. PCP use is associated with a number of risks and many believe it to be one of the most dangerous drugs of abuse.

Modification of the manufacturing process may yield chemically related analogue capable of producing psychic effects similar to PCP. Four of these substances (N-ethyl-l-phenylcyclohexylamine or PCE, l-(phenylcyclohexyl)-pyrrolidine or PCP 1-[1-(2-thienyl)-cyclohexyl]-piperdine or TCP, and 1[l-(2-thienyl) cyclohexyl] pyrrolidine or TCP have been encountered on the illicit market and have been placed in Schedule I of the CSA. LSD is also a Schedule I hallucinogen.

CANNABIS

Cannabis sativa L., the hemp plant, grows wild throughout most of the tropic and temperate regions of the world. Prior to the advent of synthetic fibers, the cannabis plant was cultivated for the tough fiber of its stem. In the United States, cannabis is legitimately grown only for scientific research. In fact, since 1980, the United States has been the only country where cannabis is licitly cultivated for scientific research.

Cannabis contains chemicals called cannabinoids that are unique to the cannabis plant. Among the cannabinoids synthesized by the plant are cannabinol, cannabidiol, cannabinolidic acids, cannabigerol, cannabichromene, and several isomers of tetrahydrocannabinol. One of these, delta-9-tetrahydrocannabinol (THC), is believed to be responsible for most of the characteristic psychoactive effects of cannabis. Research has resulted in development and marketing of dronabinol (Marinol), a product containing synthetic THC, for the control of nausea and vomiting caused by chemotherapeutic agents used in the treatment of cancer, and to stimulate appetite in AIDS patients.

Cannabis products are usually smoked. Their effects are felt within minutes, reach their peak in 10 to 30 minutes, and may linger for two or three hours. The effects experienced often depend upon the experience and expectations of the individual user as well as the activity of the drug itself. Low doses tend to induce a sense of well-being and a dreamy state of relax at on, which may be accompanied by a more vivid sense of sight, smell, taste, and hearing as well as by subtle alterations in thought formation and expression. This state of intoxication may not be noticeable to an observer. However, driving, occupational or household accidents may result from a distortion of time and space relationships and impaired coordination. Stronger doses intensify reactions. The individual may experience shifting sensory imagery, rapidly fluctuating emotions, a flight of fragmentary thoughts with disturbed associations, an altered sense of selfidentity, impaired memory, and a dulling of attention despite an illusion of heightened insight. High doses may result in image distortion, a loss of personal identity, and fantasies and hallucinations.

Three drugs that come from cannabismarijuana, hashish, and hashish oil-are currently distributed on the U.S. illicit market. Having no currently accepted medical use in treatment in the United States, they remain under Schedule I of the CSA. Today, cannabis is carefully illicitly cultivated, both indoors and out, to maximize its THC content, thereby producing the greatest possible psychoactive effect.

Marijuana

Marijuana is the most commonly used illicit drug in America today. The term marijuana, as commonly used, refers to the leaves and flowering tops of the cannabis plant.

A tobacco-like substance produced by drying the leaves and flowering tops of the cannabis plant, marijuana varies significantly in its potency, depending on the source and selection of plant materials used. The form of marijuana known as sinsemilla (Spanish, sin semilla: without seed), derived from the unpollinated female cannabis plant, is preferred for its high THC content.

Marijuana is usually smoked in the form of loosely rolled cigarettes called joints or hollowed out commercial cigars called blunts. Joints and blunts may be laced with a number of adulterants including phencyclidine (PCP), substantially altering the effects and toxicity of these products. Street names for marijuana include pot, grass, weed, Mary Jane, Acupulco Gold, and reefer.

Although marijuana grown in the U.S. was once considered inferior because of a low concentration of THC, advancements in plant selection and cultivation have resulted in highly potent domestic marijuana. In 1974, the average THC content of illicit marijuana was less than one percent; in early 1994, potency averaged 5 percent. The THC of today's sinsemilla ranges up to 17 percent.

Marijuana contains known toxins and cancer-causing chemicals which are stored in fat cells for as long as several months. Marijuana users experience the same health problems as tobacco smokers, such as bronchitis, emphysema and bronchial asthma. Some of the effects of marijuana use also include increased heart rate, dryness of the mouth, reddening of the eyes, impaired motor skills and concentration, and frequently hunger and an increased desire for sweets. Extended use increases risk to the lungs and reproductive system, as well as suppression of the immune system. Occasionally hallucinations, fantasies and paranoia are reported.

Hashish

Hashish consists of the THC-rich resinous material of the cannabis plant, which is collected, dried, and then compressed into a variety of forms, such as balls, cakes, or cookie-like sheets. Pieces are then broken off, placed in pipes and smoked. The Middle East, North Africa, and Pakistan/Afghanistan are the main sources of hashish. The THC content of hashish that reached the United States, where demand is limited, averaged 6 percent in the -1990s.

Hash Oil

The term hash oil is used by illicit drug users and dealers but is a misnomer in suggesting any resemblance to hashish. Hash oil is produced by extracting the cannabinoids from plant material with a solvent. The color and odor of the resulting extract will vary, depending on the type of solvent used. Current samples of hash oil, a viscous liquid ranging from amber to dark brown in color, average about 15 percent The. In terms of its psychoactive effect, a drop or two of this liquid on a cigarette is equal to a single "joint" of marijuana.

27
STEROIDS

Anabolic steroid abuse has become a national concern. These drugs are used illicitly by weight lifters, body builders, long distance runners, cyclists and others who claim that these drugs give them a competitive advantage and/or improve their physical appearance. Once viewed as a problem associated only with professional athletes, recent reports estimate that 5 percent to 12 percent of male high school students and 1 percent of female students have used anabolic steroids by the time they were seniors. Concerns over a growing illicit market and prevalence of abuse combined with the possibility of harmful long-term effects of steroid use, led Congress in 1991 to place anabolic steroids into Schedule III of the Controlled Substances Act (CSA).

The CSA defines anabolic steroids as any drug or hormonal substance chemically and pharmacologically related to testosterone (other than estrogens, progestins, and corticosteroids), that promotes muscle growth. Most illicit anabolic steroids are sold at gyms, competitions and through mail order operations. For the most part, these substances are smuggled into this country. Those commonly encountered on the illicit market include: boldenone (Equipoise), ethylestrenol (Maxibolin), fluoxymesterone (Halotestin), methandriol, methandrostenolone (Dianabol), methyltestosterone, nandrolone (Durabolin, Deca-Durabolin), oxandrolone (Anavar), oxymetholone (Anadrol), stanozolol (Winstrol), testosterone and trenbolone (Finajet). In addition, a number of bogus or counterfeit products are sold as anabolic steroids.

A limited number of anabolic steroids have been approved for medical and veterinary use. The primary legitimate use of these drugs in humans is for the replacement of inadequate levels of testosterone resulting from a reduction or absence of functioning testes. In veterinary practice, anabolic steroids are used to promote feed efficiency and to improve weight gain, vigor and hair coat. They are also used in veterinary practice to treat anemia and counteract tissue breakdown during illness and trauma.

When used in combination with exercise training and high protein diet, anabolic steroids can promote increased size and strength of muscles, improve endurance and decrease recovery time between workouts. They are taken orally or by intramuscular injection. Users concerned about drug tolerance often take steroids on a schedule called a cycle. A cycle is a period of between 6 and 14 weeks of steroid use followed by a period of abstinence or reduction in use. Additionally, users tend to "stack" the drugs, using multiple drugs concurrently. Although the benefits of these practices are unsubstantiated, most users feel that cycling and stacking enhance the efficiency of the drugs and limit their side effects.

Yet another mode of steroid use is "pyramiding" in which users slowly escalate steroid use (increasing the number of drugs used at one time and/or the dose and frequency of one or more steroids) reaching a peak amount at mid-cycle and gradually tapering the dose toward the end of the cycle. The escalation of steroid use can vary with different types of training. Body builders and weight lifters tend to escalate their dose to a much higher level than do long distance runners or swimmers.

The adverse effects of large doses of multiple anabolic steroids are not well established. However, there is increasing evidence of serious health problems associated with the abuse of these agents, including cardiovascular damage; liver damage and damage to reproductive Physical side effects include elevated blood pressure and cholesterol levels, severe acne, premature balding, reduced sexual function and testicular atrophy. In males, abnormal breast development (gynecomastia) can occur. In females, anabolic steroids have a mas culinizing effect resulting in more body hair, a deeper voice, smaller breasts and fewer menstrual cycles. Several of these effects are irreversible. In adolescents, abuse of these agents may prematurely stop the lengthening of bones resulting in stunted growth.

RELATED TOPICS

CLANDESTINE LABS

Drugs of abuse in the United States come from a variety of sources. Heroin and cocaine, for example, are produced in foreign countries and smuggled into the U.S. Marijuana is cultivated domestically or smuggled from foreign sources. Legitimate pharmaceuticals are diverted to the illicit market. Continuing efforts on the part of state and federal governments to reduce the amount of dangerous and illicit drugs available for abuse, combined with the demand for psychoactive substances, have contributed to the proliferation of clandestine laboratories.

Clandestine laboratories are illicit operations consisting of chemicals and equipment necessary to manufacture controlled substances. The types and numbers of laboratories seized, to a large degree, reflect regional and national trends in the types and amounts of illicit substances that are being manufactured, trafficked and abused. Clandestine laboratories have been found in remote locations like mountain cabins and rural farms. Laboratories are also being operated in single and multifamily residences in urban and suburban neighborhoods where their toxic and explosive fumes can pose a significant threat to the health and safety of local residents.

The production of some substances, such as methamphetamine, PCP, MDMA and methcathinone, requires little sophisticated equipment or knowledge of chemistry; the synthesis of other drugs such as fentanyl and LSD requires much higher levels of expertise and equipment. Some clandestine laboratory operators have little or no training in chemistry and follow underground recipes; others employ chemistry students or professionals as "cooks."

The clandestine production of all drugs is dependent on the availability of essential raw materials. The distribution, sale, import and export of certain chemicals which are important to the manufacture of common illicitly produced substances have been regulated since the enactment of the Chemical Diversion and Trafficking Act of 1988. Enforcement of this and similar state laws has had a significant impact on the availability of chemicals to the clandestine laboratory.

INHALANTS

Inhalants are a chemically diverse group of psychoactive substances composed of organic solvents and volatile substances commonly found in adhesives, lighter fluids, cleaning fluids and paint products. Their easy accessibility, low cost and ease of concealment make inhalants, for many, one of the first substances abused. While not regulated under the CSA, a few states place restrictions on the sale of these products to minors. Studies have indicated that between 5 percent and 15 percent of young people in the United States have tried inhalants, although the vast majority of these youngsters do not become chronic abusers.

Inhalants may be sniffed directly from an open container or "huffed" from a rag soaked in the substance and held to the face. Alternatively, the open container or soaked rag can be placed in a bag where the vapors can concentrate before being inhaled. Although inhalant abusers may prefer one particular substance because of odor or taste, a variety of substances may be used because of their similar effects, availability and cost. Once inhaled, the extensive capillary surface of the lungs allows rapid absorption of the substance and blood levels peak rapidly. Entry into the brain is so fast that the effects of inhalation can resemble the intensity of effects produced by intravenous injection of other psychoactive drugs.

The effects of inhalant intoxication resemble those of alcohol inebriation, with stimulation and loss of inhibition followed by depression at high doses. Users report distortion in perceptions of time and space. Many users experience headache, nausea or vomiting, slurred speech, loss of motor coordination and wheezing. A characteristic "glue sniffer's rash" around the nose and mouth may be seen. An odor of paint or solvents on clothes, skin and breath is sometimes a sign of inhalant abuse.

The chronic use of inhalants has been associated with a number of serious health problems. Glue and paint thinner sniffing in particular produce kidney abnormalities, while the solvents, toluene and trichloroethylene, cause liver toxicity. Memory impairment, attention deficits and diminished non-verbal intelligence have been associated with the abuse of inhalants. Deaths resulting from heart failure, asphyxiation or aspiration have occurred.

Controlled Substances

Drugs	CSA Schedules	Trade or Other Names	Medical Uses
Narcotics			
Heroin	I	Diacetylmorphine, Horse, Smack	None in U.S., Analgesic, Antitussive
Morphine	II	Duramorph, MS-Contin, Roxanol, Oramorph SR	Analgesic
Codeine	II, III, V	Tylenol w/Codeine, Empirin w/Codeine, Robitussin A-C, Fiorinal w/Codeine, APAP w/Codeine	Analgesic, Antitussive
Hydrocodone	II, III	Tussionex, Vicodin, Hycodan, Lorcet	Analgesic, Antitussive
Hydromorphone	II	Dilaudid	Analgesic
Oxycodone	II	Percodan, Percocet, Tylox, Roxicet, Roxicodone	Analgesic
Methadone and LAAM	I, II	Dolophine, Methadose, Levo-alpha-acetylmethadol, Levomethadyl acetate	Analgesic, Treatment of Dependence
Fentanyl and Analogs	I, II	Innovar, Sublimaze, Alfenta, Sufenta, Duragesic	Analgesic, Adjunct to Anesthesia, Anesthetic
Other Narcotics	II, III, IV, V	Percodan, Percocet, Tylox, Opium, Darvon, Talwin[2], Buprenorphine, Meperdine (Pethidine), Demerol	Analgesic, Antidiarrheal
Depressants			
Chloral Hydrate	IV	Noctec, Somnos, Felsules	Hypnotic
Barbiturates	II, III, IV	Amytal, Fiorinal, Nembutal, Seconal, Tuinal, Phenobarbital, Pentobarbital	Anesthetic, anticonvulsant, sedative hypnotic, veterinary euthanasia agent
Benzodiazepines	IV	Ativan, Dalmane, Diazepam, Librium, Xanax, Serax, Valium, Tranxene, Verstran, Versed, Halcion, Paxipam, Restoril	Antianxiety, sedative, anticonvulsant, hypnotic
Glutethimide	II	Doriden	Sedative, hypnotic
Other Depressants	I, II, III, IV	Equanil, Miltown, Noludar, Placidyl, Valmid, Methaqualone	Antianxiety, Sedative, Hypnotic
Stimulants			
Cocaine[1]	II	Coke, Flake, Snow, Crack	Local anesthetic
Amphetamine/Methamphetamine	II	Biphetamine, Desoxyn, Dexedrine, Obetrol, Ice	Attention deficit disorder, narcolepsy, weight control
Methylphenidate	II	Ritalin	Attention deficit disorder, narcolepsy
Other Stimulants	I, II, III, IV	Adipex, Didrex, Ionamin, Melfiat, Plegine, Captagon, Sanorex, Tenuate, Tepanil, Prelu-2, Preludin	Weight control
Cannabis			
Marijuana	I	Pot, Acapulco Gold, Grass, Reefer, Sinsemilla, Thai Sticks	None
Tetrahydrocannabinol	I, II	THC, Marinol	Antinauseant
Hashish and Hashish Oil	I	Hash, Hash oil	None
Hallucinogens			
LSD	I	Acid, Microdot	None
Mescaline and Peyote	I	Mescal, Buttons, Cactus	None
Amphetamine Variants	I	2, 5-DMA, STP, MDA, MDMA, Ecstasy, DOM, DOB	None
Phencyclidine and Analogs	I, II	PCE, PCPy, TCP, PCP, Hog, Loveboat, Angel Dust	None
Other Hallucinogens	I	Bufotenine, Ibogaine, DMT, DET, Psilocybin, Psilocyn	None
Anabolic Steroids			
Testosterone (Cypionate, Enanthate)	III	Depo-Testosterone, Delatestryl	Hypogonadism
Nandrolone (Decanoate, Phenpropionate)	III	Nortestosterone, Durabolin, Deca-Durabolin, Deca	Anemia, breast cancer
Oxymetholone	III	Anadrol-50	Anemia

Uses and Effects

U.S. Department of Justice
Drug Enforcement Administration

Physical Dependence	Psychological Dependence	Tolerance	Duration (Hours)	Usual Method	Possible Effects	Effects of Overdose	Withdrawal Syndrome
High	High	Yes	3-6	Injected, sniffed, smoked	Euphoria	Slow and shallow breathing	Watery eyes
High	High	Yes	3-6	Oral, smoked, injected	Drowsiness	Clammy skin	Runny nose
Moderate	Moderate	Yes	3-6	Oral, injected	Respiratory depression	Convulsions	Yawning
High	High	Yes	3-6	Oral	Constricted pupils	Coma	Loss of appetite
High	High	Yes	3-6	Oral, injected	Nausea	Possible death	Irritability
High	High	Yes	4-5	Oral			Tremors
High	High	Yes	12-72	Oral, injected			Panic
High	High	Yes	.10-72	Injected, Transdermal patch			Cramps
High-Low	High-Low	Yes	Variable	Oral, injected			Nausea
							Chills and sweating
Moderate	Moderate	Yes	5-8	Oral	Slurred speech	Shallow respiration	Anxiety
High-Mod.	High-Mod.	Yes	1-16	Oral, injected	Disorientation	Clammy skin	Insomnia
Low	Low	Yes	4-8	Oral, injected	Drunken behavior without odor of alcohol	Dilated pupils	Tremors
High	Moderate	Yes	4-8	Oral		Weak and rapid pulse	Delirium
Moderate	Moderate	Yes	4-8	Oral		Coma	Convulsions
						Possible death	Possible death
Possible	High	Yes	1-2	Sniffed, smoked, injected	Increased alertness	Agitation	Apathy
Possible	High	Yes	2-4	Oral, injected, smoked	Excitation	Increased body temperature	Long periods of sleep
Possible	High	Yes	2-4	Oral, injected	Euphoria	Hallucinations	Irritability
Possible	High	Yes	2-4	Oral, injected	Increased pulse rate & blood pressure	Convulsions	Depression
					Insomnia	Possible death	Disorientation
					Loss of appetite		
Unknown	Moderate	Yes	2-4	Smoked, oral	Euphoria	Fatigue	Occasional reports of insomnia
Unknown	Moderate	Yes	2-4	Smoked, oral	Relaxed inhibitions	Paranoia	Hyperactivity
Unknown	Moderate	Yes	2-4	Smoked, oral	Increased appetite	Possible psychosis	Decreased appetite
					Disorientation		
None	Unknown	Yes	8-12	Oral	Illusions and hallucinations	Longer	Unknown
None	Unknown	Yes	8-12	Oral	Altered perception of time and distance	More intensed 'trip' episodes	
Unknown	Unknown	Yes	Variable	Oral, injected		Psychosis	
Unknown	High	Yes	Days	Oral, smoked		Possible death	
None	Unknown	Possible	Variable	Smoked, oral, injected, sniffed			
Unknown	Unknown	Unknown	14-28 days	Injected	Virilization	Unknown	Possible depression
Unknown	Unknown	Unknown	14-21 days	Injected	Acne		
Unknown	Unknown	Unknown	24	Oral	Testicular atrophy		
					Gynecomastia		
					Aggressive behavior		
					Edema		

Designated a narcotic under the CSA   ² Not designated a narcotic under the CSA

DEPRESSANTS

Schedule II

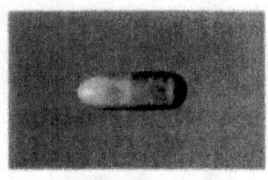

Trade Name:
Amytal Sodium
Controlled Ingredient:
amobarbital sodium
200 mg

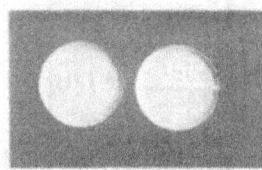

Trade Name:
Doriden
Controlled Ingredient:
glutethimide
500 mg

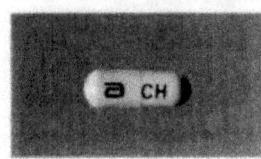

Trade Name:
Nembutal Sodium
Controlled Ingredient:
pentobarbital sodium
100 mg

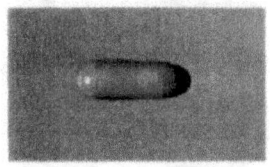

Trade Name:
Seconal Sodium
Controlled Ingredient:
secobarbital sodium
100 mg

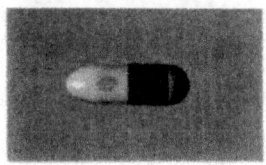

Trade Name:
Tuinal
Controlled Ingredients:
amobarbital sodium 100 mg
secobarbital sodium 100 mg

Schedule IV

Trade Name:
Ativan
Controlled Ingredient:
lorazepam
0.5 mg

Trade Name:
Ativan
Controlled Ingredient:
lorazepam
1 mg

Trade Name:
Ativan
Controlled Ingredient:
lorazepam
2 mg

Trade Name:
Centrax
Controlled Ingredient:
prazepam
5 mg

Trade Name:
Centrax
Controlled Ingredient:
prazepam 10 mg

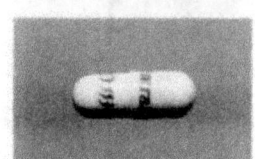

Trade Name:
Centrax
Controlled Ingredient:
prazepam 10 mg

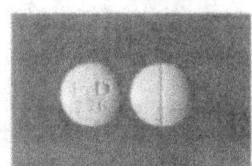

Trade Name:
Chloral Hydrate
Controlled Ingredient:
chloral hydrate
500 mg

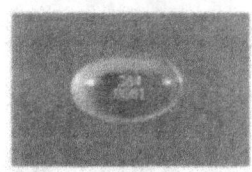

Trade Name:
Dalmane
Controlled Ingredient:
flurazepam hydrochloride
15 mg

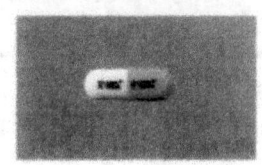

Trade Name:
Dalmane
Controlled Ingredient:
flurazepam hydrochloride
30 mg

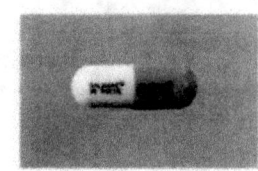

Trade Name:
Equanil
Controlled Ingredient:
meprobamate
200 mg

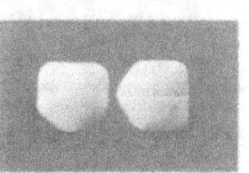

Trade Name:
Equanil
Controlled Ingredient:
meprobamate
400 mg

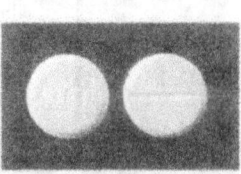

Trade Name:
Halcion
Controlled Ingredient:
triazolam
0.25 mg

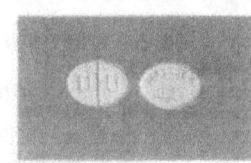

DEPRESSANTS

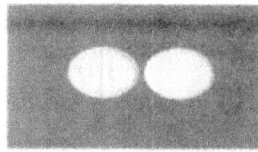
Trade Name:
Halcion
Controlled Ingredient:
triazolam
0.5 mg

Trade Name:
Restoril
Controlled Ingredient:
temazepam
15 mg
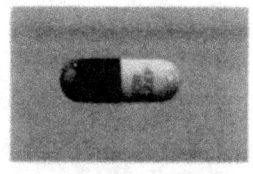

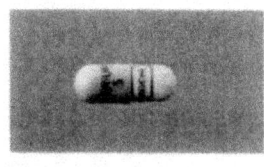
Trade Name:
Librium
Controlled Ingredient:
chlordiazepoxide hydrochloride
5 mg

Trade Name:
Restoril
Controlled Ingredient:
temazepam
30 mg
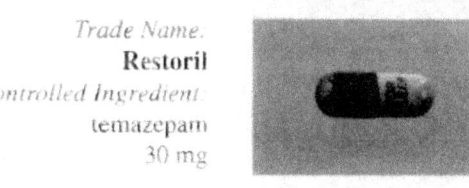

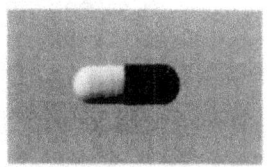
Trade Name:
Librium
Controlled Ingredient:
chlordiazepoxide hydrochloride
10 mg

Trade Name:
Serax
Controlled Ingredient:
oxazepam
10 mg
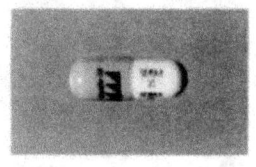

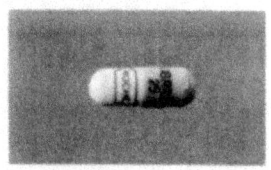
Trade Name:
Librium
Controlled Ingredient:
chlordiazepoxide hydrochloride
25 mg

Trade Name:
Serax
Controlled Ingredient:
oxazepam
15 mg
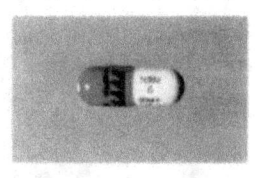

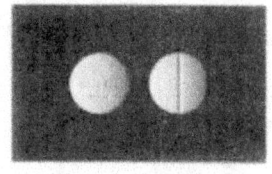
Trade Name:
Miltown 400
Controlled Ingredient:
meprobamate
400 mg

Trade Name:
Serax
Controlled Ingredient:
oxazepam 15 mg
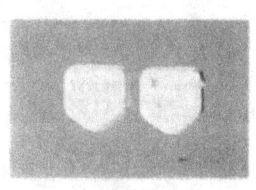

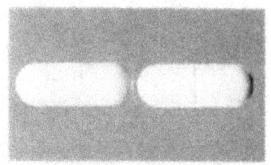
Trade Name:
Miltown 600
Controlled Ingredient:
meprobamate
600 mg

Trade Name:
Serax
Controlled Ingredient:
oxazepam
30 mg
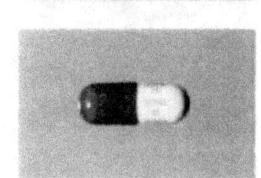

Trade Name:
Placidyl
Controlled Ingredient:
ethchlorvynol
200 mg

Trade Name:
Tranxene
Controlled Ingredient:
clorazepate dipotassium
3.75 mg
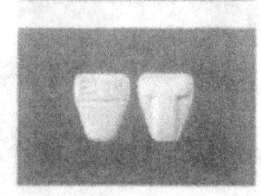

Trade Name:
Placidyl
Controlled Ingredient:
ethchlorvynol
500 mg

Trade Name:
Tranxene
Controlled Ingredient:
clorazepate dipotassium
7.5 mg
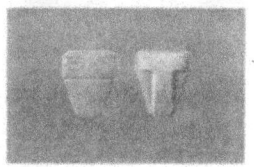

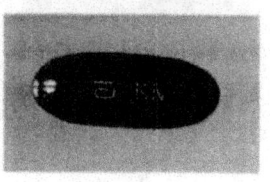
Trade Name:
Placidyl
Controlled Ingredient:
ethchlorvynol
750 mg

Trade Name:
Tranxene
Controlled Ingredient:
clorazepate dipotassium
15 mg

DEPRESSANTS

Trade Name:
Valium
Controlled Ingredient:
diazepam
2 mg

Trade Name:
Valium
Controlled Ingredient:
diazepam
5 mg

Trade Name:
Valium
Controlled Ingredient:
diazepam
10 mg

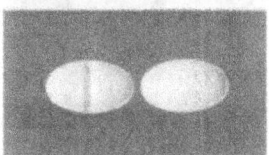

Trade Name:
Xanax
Controlled Ingredient:
alprazolam
0.25 mg

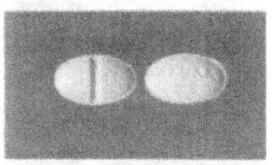

Trade Name:
Xanax
Controlled Ingredient:
alprazolam
0.5 mg

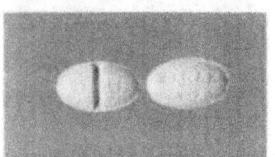

Trade Name:
Xanax
Controlled Ingredient:
alprazolam
1 mg

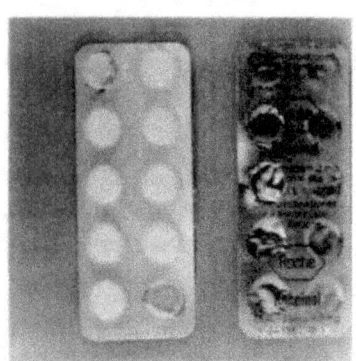

Rohyphnol contains the controlled ingredient flunitrazepam hydrochloride. Pictured here is a 2-mg tablet with packaging. "Roofies," as they are known on the street, are sold inexpensively in Mexico. They are smuggled into the United States where they have recently become a problem among American teens. The problem is rapidly spreading from the American southwest to other parts of the United States.